# 88 Polynesian Recipes

## *(88 Polynesian Recipes - Volume 1)*

Kara Quinn

# Content

# 88 Awesome Polynesian Recipes

***

## 1. Banana Cassava Cake

*Serving: 4-6 serving(s) | Prep: 15mins | Ready in:*

### Ingredients

- 1 tablespoon sugar
- 1 cup coconut cream (be sure to use coconut cream, not coconut milk)
- 4 mashed bananas
- 1 1/2-2 lbs fresh cassava, peeled and grated

### Direction

- Preheat the oven 350 F and lightly oil an 8 inch square cake pan.
- Beat the coconut cream and sugar together.
- Add the mashed bananas and mix thoroughly.
- Add the grated cassava and mix thoroughly.
- Pour into cake pan and bake for about 45 minutes until the top is a golden colour.

### Nutrition Information

- Calories: 531.7
- Cholesterol: 0
- Sodium: 62
- Fiber: 7.8
- Saturated Fat: 11.9
- Sugar: 25
- Total Carbohydrate: 101.1
- Protein: 5.6
- Total Fat: 14

## 2. Big Kahuna Burger

*Serving: 4 serving(s) | Prep: 15mins | Ready in:*

### Ingredients

- Burger
- 1 lb ground beef
- 2 tablespoons teriyaki sauce
- 1 tablespoon grill seasoning (store-bought or try Grill Seasoning)
- 4 pineapple rings (canned or fresh)
- 4 pieces bacon, cooked until crisp
- 4 slices monterey jack cheese
- 4 kaiser rolls
- Spicy cilantro mayo
- 1/3 cup mayonnaise
- 1 teaspoon sriracha chili-garlic sauce
- 1 tablespoon cilantro, finely chopped

### Direction

- Using your hands, gently mix the ground meat with the teriyaki and grill seasoning in a medium bowl. Be careful not to overwork the mixture as that can toughen the meat. Divide into four quarter-pound patties.
- Grill pineapple slices for approximately 1 minute on each side on your grill of choice.
- Grill burgers until desired doneness.
- Place a piece of bacon on each and then top with a piece of jack cheese.
- Top with a grilled pineapple slice and serve on Kaiser Rolls spread with Spicy Cilantro Mayo.
- Spicy Cilantro Mayo: Mix all together in a small bowl and use as condiment on Big Kahuna Burgers.

### Nutrition Information

- Calories: 678.3
- Sodium: 1086.7
- Sugar: 11.9
- Cholesterol: 112.6
- Protein: 35.7

- Total Fat: 38.2
- Fiber: 2.5
- Total Carbohydrate: 47.4
- Saturated Fat: 14.5

- Saturated Fat: 11.2
- Total Carbohydrate: 61.7
- Cholesterol: 0
- Fiber: 9.3

## 3. Boiled Taro With Coconut Milk

*Serving: 4-6 serving(s) | Prep: 15mins | Ready in:*

### Ingredients

- 1 (2 -3 lb) taro root
- 1 teaspoon salt
- water
- 1 (8 ounce) can unsweetened coconut milk

### Direction

- Scrub the outside of the taro.
- Place in a pot with enough water to half cover the taro.
- Cover and boil for about 1 1/2 hours, or until tender. (Make sure the taro is cooked very well, for the starches can irritate and scratch the throat if not cooked through completely).
- Remove and cool.
- Peel away the outside skin and chop taro into large cubes. (Cooked taro at this point can be mashed and formed into cakes that are delicious sautéed with butter).
- Place the coconut milk and the taro cubes into a saucepan and heat thoroughly.
- There should be enough milk to just cover the taro.
- Taste during cooking to see if taro needs more salt.

### Nutrition Information

- Calories: 369.8
- Sodium: 614
- Sugar: 0.9
- Protein: 4.6
- Total Fat: 13

## 4. Bora Bora (Non Alcoholic)

*Serving: 1 serving(s) | Prep: 2mins | Ready in:*

### Ingredients

- 2 1/2 ounces pineapple juice
- 1 1/2 ounces passion fruit juice
- 1/4 ounce lemon juice
- 1/4 ounce grenadine
- pineapple slice, garnish
- red maraschino cherry, garnish
- ice

### Direction

- Mix juices and pour into tall glass filled with ice.
- Garnish with a slice of pineapple and a maraschino cherry.

### Nutrition Information

- Calories: 58.4
- Saturated Fat: 0
- Sodium: 3.4
- Fiber: 0.2
- Total Carbohydrate: 14.4
- Cholesterol: 0
- Protein: 0.3
- Total Fat: 0.1
- Sugar: 10.6

## 5. Bora Bora Nui

*Serving: 20 glasses | Prep: 20mins | Ready in:*

## Ingredients

- 2 cups white rum
- 2 cups dark rum
- 2/3 cup Cointreau liqueur
- 6 cups blood orange juice
- 6 cups pineapple juice
- 2/3 cup simple syrup
- 1 vanilla bean
- 2 limes

## Direction

- Mix together the rums, Cointreau, fruit juices and simple syrup.
- Split the vanilla bean down the middle and scoop out the seeds. Add these to the mixture along with the bean.
- Wash the limes thoroughly. Cut one into quarters and add to the punch. Juice the other lime and add to the punch. Mix well.
- Chill the punch for 6 hours to allow the flavors to blend.

## Nutrition Information

- Calories: 178
- Cholesterol: 0
- Sodium: 2.8
- Fiber: 0.5
- Sugar: 13.8
- Total Carbohydrate: 18.1
- Protein: 0.8
- Total Fat: 0.2
- Saturated Fat: 0

## 6. Breakfast Club Smoothie

*Serving: 4 serving(s) | Prep: 10mins | Ready in:*

## Ingredients

- 2 -3 bananas, overripe
- 10 strawberries, too tart
- 3/4 cup fresh pineapple, on the sour side
- 2 cups low-fat plain yogurt

## Direction

- Cut fruit in large chunks (just de-stem strawberries).
- Puree in blender until smooth and pink.
- Be refreshed as your bad fruit is redeemed!

## Nutrition Information

- Calories: 201
- Sodium: 72.2
- Sugar: 34.6
- Protein: 6.3
- Total Fat: 1.6
- Saturated Fat: 0.9
- Fiber: 2.5
- Total Carbohydrate: 42.8
- Cholesterol: 4.9

## 7. Butter Rum Pineapple Upside Down Cake

*Serving: 8 big slices, 8 serving(s) | Prep: 15mins | Ready in:*

## Ingredients

- 6 pineapple rings, reserve juice (fresh or canned)
- 1/2 cup spiced rum (such as Captain Morgan's)
- 1/4 lb butter
- 1 cup firmly packed brown sugar
- 1/2 cup chopped macadamia nuts
- 1/4 cup reserved pineapple juice (can include some of the rum that was used to soak the pineapple)
- 3 eggs, separated
- 1 cup granulated sugar
- 1 cup all-purpose white flour
- 1/4 teaspoon salt
- 1 teaspoon baking powder
- 6 maraschino cherries, halves (optional)

## Direction

- Marinate pineapple rings in rum overnight.
- Preheat oven to 350 degrees.
- Melt the butter and brown sugar in a large iron skillet (at least 12"), or other heavy, oven-proof pan.
- Arrange the marinated pineapple rings in the bottom of the pan in a single layer and simmer slowly over low heat in the melted butter and sugar until the cake batter is ready to go into the pan.
- Mix the granulated sugar, reserved pineapple juice and egg yolks in a large bowl.
- Sift the flour, baking powder and salt in a separate bowl.
- Beat egg whites until peaks form.
- Quickly mix flour mixture into the sugar and egg mixture until well blended. Gently fold in egg whites.
- Place one cherry half upside down in the middle of each pineapple ring. Sprinkle chopped macadamia nuts evenly over the rings, gently spoon the batter over the pineapple rings and macadamia nuts.
- Bake for 20-25 minutes, or until a toothpick comes out clean.
- Let the cake cool until it is just warm to the touch, then invert over a large plate.
- Serve warm or at room temperature.

## Nutrition Information

- Calories: 514.8
- Cholesterol: 100.2
- Total Fat: 19.9
- Sodium: 255.6
- Fiber: 2
- Total Carbohydrate: 74.6
- Protein: 5.2
- Saturated Fat: 8.9
- Sugar: 59.1

## 8. Calypso Shrimp Skewers

*Serving: 30 shrimp, 15 serving(s) | Prep: 15mins | Ready in:*

## Ingredients

- 1/3 cup honey
- 1 teaspoon fresh ginger
- 2/3 cup shredded coconut
- 2/3 cup finely chopped peanuts
- 12 ounces medium shrimp, peeled and deveined
- 3 ounces thinly sliced prosciutto
- 7 ounces creme fraiche
- 1 teaspoon finely shredded lime peel
- lime juice

## Direction

- Cut prosciutto into 1/2 inch wide by 7 inch long strips.
- Soak thirty 6-inch skewers in water for 30 minutes.
- Meanwhile, in a shallow dish combine honey and ginger and set aside.
- In another shallow dish combine peanuts and coconut and set aside.
- Drain skewers. Thread shrimp lengthwise on skewers at tail end until they are straight.
- Brush each shrimp with honey mixture.
- Roll in coconut mixture wrap a piece of prosciutto around each shrimp.
- If grilling, cook shrimp until opaque.
- If cooking in oven, preheat to 375 degrees and bake 4 to 6 minutes.
- Stir together crème fraiche, lime peel, and enough lime juice to make the desired consistency.

## Nutrition Information

- Calories: 142.4
- Total Carbohydrate: 9.8
- Total Fat: 9.8
- Saturated Fat: 4.8
- Sodium: 146.7

- Sugar: 8.2
- Protein: 5.2
- Fiber: 0.8
- Cholesterol: 46.9

## 9. Carrots Polynesian

*Serving: 4 serving(s) | Prep: 5mins | Ready in:*

### Ingredients

- 1 cup water
- 1 teaspoon salt
- 2 cups carrots, thinly sliced
- 8 ounces crushed pineapple, undrained
- 1 tablespoon cornstarch, blended with 2 Tbsp. water

### Direction

- Bring water and salt to a boil; add carrots; cover and cook 10 minutes until crisp tender.
- Stir in pineapple; cook 5 minutes.
- Add cornstarch. Cook and stir until thickened and clear.

### Nutrition Information

- Calories: 67.9
- Protein: 0.8
- Total Fat: 0.2
- Sugar: 11.2
- Cholesterol: 0
- Saturated Fat: 0
- Sodium: 628
- Fiber: 2.3
- Total Carbohydrate: 16.9

## 10. Chicken Kelaguin

*Serving: 6 serving(s) | Prep: 20mins | Ready in:*

### Ingredients

- 3 cups coconut, fresh and shredded
- 4 cups cooked barbecued chicken, diced
- 1/4 cup onion, chopped
- 1/4 cup lemon juice
- 1/16 teaspoon salt (optional)
- 1 jalapeno pepper, seeded and chopped
- 1/4 cup green pepper, optional for garnish

### Direction

- Remove excess juice from the shredded coconut by firmly squeezing; add coconut to chicken.
- Add onion, lemon juice, salt, and pepper.
- If the mixture seems too dry, add either more lemon juice or water, depending upon your family's preferences concerning lemon.
- Marinate for 3 hours.
- Garnish with green pepper.

### Nutrition Information

- Calories: 443.8
- Total Carbohydrate: 12
- Sodium: 86.2
- Fiber: 7.2
- Sugar: 3.9
- Cholesterol: 70
- Protein: 26.4
- Total Fat: 33.7
- Saturated Fat: 26

## 11. Chilled Hearts Of Palm With Asparagus And Coconut Lime Dressing

*Serving: 5 serving(s) | Prep: 15mins | Ready in:*

### Ingredients

- 20 asparagus spears, blanched and chilled
- 1 lb hearts of palm, thinly sliced

- 1 japanese cucumber, thinly sliced
- 1/2 lb mixed baby greens
- 1/4 cup roasted macadamia nuts, chopped (garnish)
- Coconut Lime Dressing
- 1/2 cup coconut milk
- 1/4 cup rice wine vinegar
- 1/8 cup lime juice
- 3 tablespoons honey
- 1 cup canola oil
- salt and pepper, to taste

## Direction

- In a large bowl combine asparagus, hearts of palm, cucumber and mixed baby greens.
- In a medium-size bowl combine coconut milk, rice wine vinegar, lime juice and honey. Stir with a wire whisk while slowly adding canola oil in a steady stream. Once all the oil is incorporated, season to taste with salt and pepper. Add dressing to salad, and toss gently.
- To serve, sprinkle macadamia nuts on each serving.

## Nutrition Information

- Calories: 626.7
- Sugar: 27.8
- Total Carbohydrate: 36.4
- Cholesterol: 0
- Protein: 5.1
- Total Fat: 54.3
- Saturated Fat: 8.8
- Fiber: 4.4
- Sodium: 408

## 12. Cilantro Vinaigrette

*Serving: 1 cup | Prep: 10mins | Ready in:*

## Ingredients

- 1/3 cup fresh lime juice
- 4 garlic cloves, peeled
- 2 tablespoons fresh cilantro, chopped (or to taste)
- 2 tablespoons fresh Italian parsley, chopped
- 2 teaspoons chili powder
- 1 1/2 teaspoons ground cumin
- 1/4 teaspoon dried oregano
- 1/8 teaspoon cayenne pepper
- 3/4 teaspoon salt
- ground black pepper, to taste
- 1 cup canola oil (or peanut oil-do not use olive oil)

## Direction

- Place all ingredients except oil in a food processor or blender. Process until combined.
- With the machine running, slowly pour oil through opening in lid or feeder tube and process until emulsified.
- Taste for seasoning (and more cilantro or cayenne if needed).
- Pour into a glass jar with lid and refrigerate for at least 1 hour but preferably overnight.

## Nutrition Information

- Calories: 1996.8
- Cholesterol: 0
- Sodium: 1846.9
- Fiber: 3.3
- Total Carbohydrate: 15.7
- Protein: 2.7
- Total Fat: 219.7
- Saturated Fat: 16.3
- Sugar: 2.1

## 13. Coco Chaos

*Serving: 1 serving(s) | Prep: 5mins | Ready in:*

## Ingredients

- 30 ml melon liqueur
- 15 ml vodka
- 60 ml coconut cream
- 30 ml vanilla ice cream
- ice cube

## Direction

- Place all the ingredients in a blender with a small handful of ice.
- Blend, pour, and drink.

## Nutrition Information

- Calories: 331.6
- Saturated Fat: 12.6
- Total Carbohydrate: 43.3
- Sugar: 41.7
- Cholesterol: 7.4
- Protein: 1.4
- Total Fat: 13.9
- Sodium: 40.2
- Fiber: 0.3

## 14. Coconut Ahi Seviche Ceviche

*Serving: 8-12 serving(s) | Prep: 20mins | Ready in:*

## Ingredients

- 10 ounces coconut milk
- 1 tablespoon ginger, chopped
- 1 tablespoon horseradish, grated
- 12 ounces sashimi-grade ahi, cubed into medium pieces
- 1 tomatoes, seeded and diced
- salt and pepper, to taste
- 1 small red onion, julienned
- 1 scallion, julienned

## Direction

- In a saucepan, bring coconut milk, ginger and horseradish to a boil and reduce by a quarter.

- Strain out ginger and horseradish through fine sieve and allow coconut milk to cool.
- In a mixing bowl, combine raw tuna and tomato with coconut sauce.
- Season with salt and pepper.
- Place in a serving bowl and garnish with julienned onion and scallion.
- Yields 3 to 4 salad serving or 8 to 12 Pu Pu (hors d'oeuvres) servings.

## Nutrition Information

- Calories: 141.5
- Total Fat: 9.7
- Sodium: 28.8
- Fiber: 0.5
- Cholesterol: 16.3
- Protein: 11.1
- Saturated Fat: 7.3
- Sugar: 1
- Total Carbohydrate: 3.2

## 15. Coconut Cream Pudding With Cinnamon

*Serving: 10 1/2 cup servings, 8 serving(s) | Prep: 5mins | Ready in:*

## Ingredients

- 3 large eggs, beaten
- 4 cups milk
- 1/3 cup granulated sugar
- 2 teaspoons vanilla
- 1 teaspoon ground cinnamon
- 1/4 teaspoon salt
- 1 1/2 tablespoons cornstarch
- 4 tablespoons cold water
- 3/4 cup shredded sweetened coconut

## Direction

- In heavy 2 quart saucepan, add milk, beaten eggs, sugar, vanilla, cinnamon and salt.

- Use a large whisk to mix and stir.
- Heat on medium heat, and whisk.
- It will start to become a custard like consistency. Cook a few minutes.
- Take off heat.
- Mix cornstarch with water in small bowl.
- Add to pudding mixture.
- Turn heat on low and cook until thickened and creamy. Use a whisk to mix and stir while cooking.
- Fold in coconut.
- Cool in the refrigerator.
- Serve as a pudding with whipped cream and cherries on top or pour into a baked pie crust shell and chill until serving.
- Note: To make a deep dish pie, add 1 1/2 cups of Cool Whip or Whipped Cream to pudding before filling the pie crust.
- Note: Pumpkin pie spice may be substituted for cinnamon if you wish.

## Nutrition Information

- Calories: 180.2
- Protein: 6.6
- Total Fat: 8.6
- Fiber: 0.5
- Sugar: 11.6
- Total Carbohydrate: 19.2
- Cholesterol: 96.4
- Saturated Fat: 5.3
- Sodium: 176.9

## 16. Coconut Oil On Toast

*Serving: 1 toast, 1 serving(s) | Prep: 1mins | Ready in:*

### Ingredients

- 1 toast, of your choice
- 1 fair amount coconut oil

### Direction

- Make sure that the toast is toast, not bread, by putting it in the toaster before you put the coconut oil on it.
- Spread coconut oil on the toast.
- Serve warm (or just eat).

## Nutrition Information

- Calories: 0
- Saturated Fat: 0
- Fiber: 0
- Total Carbohydrate: 0
- Cholesterol: 0
- Protein: 0
- Total Fat: 0
- Sodium: 0
- Sugar: 0

## 17. Coconut Popsicle

*Serving: 12 serving(s) | Prep: 10mins | Ready in:*

### Ingredients

- 1 (15 ounce) can coconut milk
- 1/2 cup sugar
- 1 cup ice cube
- 1/2 cup heavy cream
- 1/2 cup milk
- 1/4 teaspoon imitation coconut extract
- 2 tablespoons unsweetened dried shredded coconut (optional)

### Direction

- Drain the coconut water off the full fat coconut milk. Use the cream of the coconut milk. Put in pan and add sugar. Stir and heat just until sugar is dissolved. Add ice cubes and stir until ice cubes melted and coconut mixture is cooled down. Add heavy cream, milk, coconut flavoring, and coconut flakes. Pour in Popsicle molds and freeze.

## Nutrition Information

- Calories: 205.3
- Total Fat: 10.1
- Fiber: 0.1
- Sugar: 27.4
- Protein: 1
- Saturated Fat: 8.2
- Sodium: 22.8
- Total Carbohydrate: 28.8
- Cholesterol: 15

## 18. Coconut Shrimp With Guava Sweet And Sour Sauce

*Serving: 12 jumbo shrimp, 2 serving(s) | Prep: 15mins | Ready in:*

## Ingredients

- 12 jumbo shrimp, peeled, deveined and butterflied
- 1 cup coconut flakes
- 1 cup panko breadcrumbs
- 3 eggs, Beaten
- 1 cup flour
- 3 cups frying oil
- 1 cup guava, concentrate
- 1/2 cup rice vinegar or 1/2 cup white vinegar
- 1/2 cup pineapple juice
- 1/2 cup sugar
- 1 tablespoon cornstarch
- 1 tablespoon water

## Direction

- Pre-heat oil to 350 degrees in medium frying pan.
- In a medium, mixing bowl, combine coconut and panko.
- Dredge shrimp in flour, then in the egg mixture, then in the panko and coconut mix, pressing down firmly to ensure proper breading.
- Fry shrimp until golden brown being sure not to burn. (The coconut contains a high sugar content, which may burn quickly.)
- In a separate saucepan, combine sugar, vinegar, and pineapple juice. Bring to a boil and allow sugar to incorporate into the sauce.
- Add guava concentrate and allow to boil.
- Mix the cornstarch and water to make a slurry. (You may use cornstarch slurry to thicken the sauce to the correct consistency. The sauce should be able to coat a spoon.)
- You may use the sauce as a dip or simply pour the sauce over the shrimp when ready to serve.

## Nutrition Information

- Calories: 4027.7
- Total Fat: 351.8
- Saturated Fat: 57
- Fiber: 11.2
- Total Carbohydrate: 179.5
- Cholesterol: 490.7
- Protein: 48.8
- Sodium: 1578.4
- Sugar: 80

## 19. Dan's Famous To Die For Polynesian Ham

*Serving: 6-8 serving(s) | Prep: 20mins | Ready in:*

## Ingredients

- honey-roasted ham or smoked ham, with bone in
- 1 whole clove
- 2 tablespoons butter
- 2 tablespoons prepared horseradish
- 2 tablespoons mustard
- 1 cup brown sugar
- 1/2 cup maple syrup
- 1/4 teaspoon sugar
- 1/4 teaspoon cinnamon

- 1/4 teaspoon allspice
- 1 tablespoon vinegar
- 2 tablespoons lemon juice
- 1/4 cup orange juice

## Direction

- I swore I'd never share this recipe, but here goes.
- Make slices on the whole ham 1/4" deep.
- Insert whole cloves 1 inch apart on whole ham.
- Mix all above ingredients (except for cloves) in a pot and heat on stove on low till sauce is warm.
- Preheat oven to 325 degrees.
- Place ham in a large roasting pan.
- Pour most of sauce on ham (save about 1/4 cup).
- Place ham in oven with foil loosely on top.
- Baste with the sauce in roasting pan every 45 minutes (5-7 lb. Ham takes about 2 hours to cook).
- Slice ham.
- When ham is sliced brush on the saved 1/4 cup sauce (don't use the roasting pan sauce. It's too greasy).
- Serve immediately.
- The only problem with this recipe is that you will be asked to make it for every family function.
- Enjoy!

## Nutrition Information

- Calories: 255.4
- Sodium: 116
- Cholesterol: 10.2
- Total Fat: 4.1
- Saturated Fat: 2.5
- Fiber: 0.4
- Sugar: 53
- Total Carbohydrate: 56.5
- Protein: 0.4

## 20. Dhal Soup

*Serving: 8 serving(s) | Prep: 10mins | Ready in:*

## Ingredients

- 2 cups dried split yellow peas
- 12 cups water
- 4 tablespoons ghee
- 1 -2 chili pepper, minced
- 1 teaspoon cumin seed
- 1 1/2 medium onions, diced
- 8 garlic cloves, thinly sliced
- 1 1/2 teaspoons turmeric
- salt
- cilantro, chopped for garnish

## Direction

- Rinse split peas and place in a pot with the water.
- Bring to a boil and simmer for 30 minutes, skim occasionally.
- Heat the ghee in a frying pan, brown the chili and cumin seeds, then add onion and garlic.
- Sauté until onions are golden brown on the edges then add turmeric.
- Add spicy butter mixture to split peas, simmer for about 1 hour.
- Season with salt to taste.
- If the soup appears to be too thick, add more water for a medium-thick consistency.
- Fold in the cilantro leaves before serving.
- Serve hot.

## Nutrition Information

- Calories: 241.4
- Total Fat: 7.1
- Saturated Fat: 4.1
- Sodium: 20.6
- Protein: 12.7
- Fiber: 13.2
- Sugar: 5.2
- Total Carbohydrate: 33.5

- Cholesterol: 16.4

## 21. Dr. Polynesian's Wet 'n' Wild Barbecue Sauce

*Serving: 2 1/2-3 cups | Prep: 15mins | Ready in:*

## Ingredients

- 1 cup brown sugar style barbecue sauce
- 1 cup crushed pineapple in juice
- 1 1/2 teaspoons yellow mustard
- 1 tablespoon grated ginger
- 1 tablespoon light molasses
- 1 tablespoon soy sauce
- 1 tablespoon cider vinegar
- 1 tablespoon mirin
- 1 teaspoon liquid smoke
- 2 teaspoons dark sesame oil or 2 teaspoons hot sesame oil

## Direction

- Simmer sauce ingredients over low heat 30 minutes.
- Use sauce immediately, or allow to cool and puree for a smoother texture.

## Nutrition Information

- Calories: 282.3
- Protein: 1.5
- Sodium: 1324.9
- Sugar: 45.2
- Cholesterol: 0
- Total Fat: 4.2
- Saturated Fat: 0.6
- Fiber: 1.9
- Total Carbohydrate: 60.3

## 22. Easy Polynesian Marinade

*Serving: 2 1/2 cups, 4 serving(s) | Prep: 10mins | Ready in:*

## Ingredients

- 1 cup sugar
- 1 cup soy sauce
- 1 cup white vinegar
- 1 -2 teaspoon minced garlic (optional)
- lots black pepper

## Direction

- Mix all ingredients in a bowl until the sugar dissolves. Add chicken, fish, or any other meat and marinate several hours or overnight.

## Nutrition Information

- Calories: 249.2
- Protein: 7.6
- Total Fat: 0.1
- Fiber: 0.6
- Sugar: 51.4
- Total Carbohydrate: 54.6
- Cholesterol: 0
- Saturated Fat: 0
- Sodium: 4025.4

## 23. Fijian Potato Omelette

*Serving: 6 serving(s) | Prep: 10mins | Ready in:*

## Ingredients

- 2 tablespoons extra virgin olive oil
- 1 onion, peeled and finely chopped
- 2 teaspoons mustard seeds
- 2 teaspoons cumin seeds
- 1 teaspoon fennel seed, crushed
- 1 teaspoon curry powder
- 1 pinch cayenne
- 2 garlic cloves, peeled and crushed

- 1 teaspoon gingerroot, peeled and minced
- 4 medium-large potatoes, peeled, diced and cooked
- 1 cup peas, thawed if using frozen
- 6 eggs
- 1 teaspoon salt
- 1/2 teaspoon fresh ground black pepper

## Direction

- Heat oil in a large, heavy fry pan and gently fry onion, spices, garlic and ginger over a low heat for about 10 minutes.
- Remove from heat and mix in potatoes and peas.
- Beat eggs in a large bowl.
- Add the spiced vegetables to the eggs and combine evenly.
- Season well.
- Lightly re-oil the pan. Pour mixture back into the pan and cook over a very low heat for 8-10 minutes, taking care the omelette doesn't burn.
- As it cooks, heat grill. To finish off, place omelette under grill until it puffs up and turns golden.
- Stand for 5 minutes before turning out.
- Allow to cool then cut into wedges.

## Nutrition Information

- Calories: 265.2
- Total Fat: 10.3
- Saturated Fat: 2.3
- Sodium: 469.6
- Fiber: 5.4
- Sugar: 4
- Total Carbohydrate: 32.8
- Cholesterol: 211.5
- Protein: 11.3

## 24. Filipino Lumpia Wrappers

*Serving: 12 serving(s) | Prep: 10mins | Ready in:*

## Ingredients

- 1 cup flour
- 1 egg
- 1 cup water

## Direction

- Mix until smooth.
- Lightly grease heated pan.
- Brush mix in heated pan.
- Lift carefully when dough begins to come away from pan.
- And set on cooling rack.
- Wrappers should be thin enough to be cooked on one side.
- You can also use a crepe pan to make this easier.

## Nutrition Information

- Calories: 44
- Cholesterol: 17.6
- Saturated Fat: 0.1
- Sodium: 6.4
- Sugar: 0.1
- Total Carbohydrate: 8
- Protein: 1.6
- Total Fat: 0.5
- Fiber: 0.3

## 25. Finadene Island Sauce For Everything

*Serving: 2 cups | Prep: 5mins | Ready in:*

## Ingredients

- 1 cup lemon juice
- 2/3 cup soy sauce
- 1 cup chopped onion
- 2 stalks green onions, chopped
- 10 -12 medium hot peppers, chopped, according to your heat preference

- OPTIONAL
- cherry tomatoes, sliced
- cucumber, sliced
- lemon, sliced

## Direction

- Make this a few hours ahead or the night before. Mix all ingredients together and store in the refrigerator until you're ready to serve!
- Pour it over rice (a standard for ALL Guamanians), over chicken, barbecue, ribs, fish, vegetables.

## Nutrition Information

- Calories: 121.3
- Total Fat: 0.5
- Sodium: 5372.1
- Fiber: 2.9
- Sugar: 8.4
- Cholesterol: 0
- Protein: 11.7
- Saturated Fat: 0.1
- Total Carbohydrate: 22.3

## 26. Giovanni's Shrimp Scampi

*Serving: 1 Dozen, 1-2 serving(s) | Prep: 15mins | Ready in:*

## Ingredients

- 12 large raw shrimp, deveined
- 1 head garlic, peeled and roughly chopped
- salt  freshly ground black pepper
- 1/4 cup clarified butter (ghee)
- 1 tablespoon flour
- 1 lemon wedge
- 2 scoops sticky white rice, for serving

## Direction

- Rinse shrimp in cool running water and lightly pat dry. Stir the shrimp, garlic, salt, pepper,

flour and butter gently together in a covered container. Allow to marinate in the fridge for at least one hour. Remove from fridge and let sit at room temperature for approximately 30 minutes.
- Heat a sauté pan over medium-high until hot. Pour contents of container into pan and sauté shrimp for about 3 minutes on each side. Once the garlic begins to brown, turn off heat. Remove the shrimp immediately and serve with the rice and lemon wedge. Spoon the extra sauce over the rice and shrimp.

## Nutrition Information

- Calories: 586.4
- Saturated Fat: 29.3
- Fiber: 1.7
- Sugar: 0.8
- Total Carbohydrate: 27.2
- Total Fat: 47.3
- Sodium: 492.2
- Cholesterol: 227.8
- Protein: 16.6

## 27. Grown Up Noodle Soup 123

*Serving: 2 serving(s) | Prep: 5mins | Ready in:*

## Ingredients

- 3 cups water
- 1 (3 ounce) package chicken-flavored ramen noodles
- 1/2 cup chicken (meat of choice)
- 1/2 cup mixed peas (vegetable of choice)
- 1/4 onion
- 2 teaspoons fresh ginger (grated or chopped)
- 3 garlic cloves, crushed
- 1/4 cup chopped cilantro
- 1/4 cup chopped green onion
- 1 tomatoes, diced

## Direction

- Cube precooked chicken, sausages or any meat of choice. Can also use raw meat.
- Add ginger, onion, garlic, and meat into a pot of water and bring to boil. If dealing with raw meat, then boil longer till meat is cooked.
- Toss in mixed peas or your favorite veggies already cubed. Again if raw veggies then let it cook first if preferable or half cooked is still fine.
- Turn off heat, open pack of ramen noodle, break into 4 parts, throw into soup along with flavour that comes with it and let it sit for about 2-3 minutes for noodles to cook.
- Dish into bowl and garnish with a handful of cilantro, green onions, and tomatoes. Enjoy hearty healthy tasty and easy to make soup.
- NB this soup can be cooked in the microwave.

## Nutrition Information

- Calories: 255.9
- Total Fat: 7.6
- Protein: 7.4
- Cholesterol: 0
- Saturated Fat: 3.3
- Sodium: 509.1
- Fiber: 3.6
- Sugar: 5
- Total Carbohydrate: 40.8

## 28. Guava Vinaigarette

*Serving: 5 serving(s) | Prep: 5mins | Ready in:*

## Ingredients

- 1 tablespoon minced red onion
- 2 tablespoons guava nectar
- 2 tablespoons red wine vinegar
- 1/8 teaspoon kosher salt
- freshly ground pepper
- 1/4 cup extra virgin olive oil

## Direction

- In a bowl, combine the onion, guava nectar, vinegar, salt and pepper. Slowly add the olive oil in a stream while constantly whisking — this will emulsify the dressing. Serve immediately tossed with mixed baby greens.

## Nutrition Information

- Calories: 96.3
- Cholesterol: 0
- Saturated Fat: 1.5
- Sugar: 0.1
- Total Carbohydrate: 0.2
- Protein: 0
- Total Fat: 10.8
- Sodium: 43.9
- Fiber: 0

## 29. Haupia Sauce

*Serving: 12 serving(s) | Prep: 5mins | Ready in:*

## Ingredients

- 1/2 cup sugar
- 1 tablespoon cornstarch
- 1/4 teaspoon salt
- 1 teaspoon coconut extract
- 1 (14 ounce) can coconut milk, shaken well before opening

## Direction

- In a saucepan, combine sugar, cornstarch and salt. Add extract and coconut milk and simmer until thickened.
- Cook or medium heat until it thickens. Serve warm over pancakes or crepes.

## Nutrition Information

- Calories: 100.8
- Total Fat: 7.1
- Saturated Fat: 6.3

- Sodium: 52.9
- Sugar: 8.3
- Total Carbohydrate: 9.9
- Cholesterol: 0
- Protein: 0.7
- Fiber: 0

## 30. Hawaiian Bread

*Serving: 1 loaf | Prep: 0S | Ready in:*

## Ingredients

- 1 package dry yeast
- 3 cups flour
- 2 tablespoons dry milk
- 1/3 cup coconut
- 1 teaspoon salt
- 3 tablespoons sugar
- 1/4 cup oil
- 1 (8 ounce) package cream cheese, at room temperature
- 2 teaspoons coconut extract
- 1 (8 ounce) can pineapple chunks, drained (reserve juice)
- 1/4 cup pineapple juice (reserved)

## Direction

- Place all ingredients in bread machine on sweet bread setting, using darker than normal crust setting.
- Dough will appear dry until the cream cheese and pineapple become well blended.

## Nutrition Information

- Calories: 3257.5
- Sugar: 86.2
- Total Carbohydrate: 389.1
- Cholesterol: 264.4
- Total Fat: 160.2
- Saturated Fat: 76.3
- Sodium: 3079.1

- Fiber: 18.1
- Protein: 65.7

## 31. Hawaiian Coconut Shrimp With Sweet And Sour Soy Sauce

*Serving: 8 serving(s) | Prep: 5mins | Ready in:*

## Ingredients

- 24 large shrimp, peeled
- 1/2 cup unbleached white flour
- sea salt and freshly ground black pepper
- 2 egg whites
- 3 cups desiccated coconut
- 6 tablespoons lard or 6 tablespoons goose fat
- 1 cup sweet and sour sauce (recipe follows)
- Soy Sauce
- 2 garlic cloves
- 2 tablespoons coconut or 2 tablespoons maple sugar
- 2 tablespoons fresh limes or 2 tablespoons lemon juice
- 1/2 cup warm water
- 7 tablespoons naturally fermented soy sauce
- cayenne pepper (optional)

## Direction

- Mix flour, sea salt and pepper on a large plate.
- Lightly beat egg whites in a medium bowl.
- Spread coconut on another large plate.
- Dip shrimp in flour then in egg whites.
- Roll each shrimp in coconut until well covered.
- Heat lard in a large cast-iron skillet over medium high heat and fry shrimp until browned and crispy, about 5 minutes on each side.
- Soy Sauce:
- Mix all ingredients and stir until sugar is dissolved.
- Makes 1 cup.
- Serve shrimp with sweet and sour soy sauce.

## Nutrition Information

- Calories: 331.7
- Sodium: 1119.3
- Fiber: 2.1
- Total Carbohydrate: 29
- Saturated Fat: 13.1
- Sugar: 19.4
- Cholesterol: 41.3
- Protein: 8.1
- Total Fat: 20.9

## 32. Hawaiian Glazed Chicken

*Serving: 6 serving(s) | Prep: 24hours | Ready in:*

### Ingredients

- 1 tablespoon sambal oelek
- 1 tablespoon ginger, minced
- 2 tablespoons minced garlic
- 1/4 cup white sugar
- 1/4 cup oyster sauce
- 1/2 cup soy sauce
- 1/4 cup water
- 2 tablespoons sesame seeds
- 2 tablespoons green onions, sliced thin
- 6 boneless skinless chicken breast halves
- mae ploy sweet chili sauce (or Thai Sweet Chili Sauce)

### Direction

- For the marinade, combine first 9 ingredients and mix well. Taste for seasoning, if too salty, add additional water.
- To a zip lock bag, add chicken breasts and the prepared marinade. Squeeze out excess air and marinate for up to 24 hours. Discard marinade.
- Prepare grill and cook slowly with indirect heat until fully cooked about 5-8 minutes depending on thickness. In the last few

minutes brush with chili sauce for additional glazing or serve sauce on the side for dipping.

## Nutrition Information

- Calories: 212.3
- Total Fat: 4.7
- Fiber: 0.8
- Total Carbohydrate: 13.4
- Cholesterol: 75.5
- Saturated Fat: 0.9
- Sodium: 1813.8
- Sugar: 8.8
- Protein: 28.6

## 33. Horseradish Vinaigrette (Tahiti)

*Serving: 1 1/2 cups | Prep: 5mins | Ready in:*

### Ingredients

- 1 tablespoon grated fresh horseradish
- 1 teaspoon minced garlic
- 2 teaspoons Dijon mustard
- 1 teaspoon sambal oelek chili paste
- 3 tablespoons honey
- 4 tablespoons soy sauce
- 3 tablespoons lime juice
- 3/4 cup peanut oil
- salt

### Direction

- Combine horseradish, garlic, mustard, sambal, honey, soy sauce, and lime juice in a bowl.
- Stirring constantly, slowly drizzle in oil until blended.
- Add salt to taste.

## Nutrition Information

- Calories: 1127.5
- Total Fat: 108.3
- Sodium: 2761.3

- Sugar: 35.9
- Protein: 5.8
- Saturated Fat: 18.3
- Fiber: 1
- Total Carbohydrate: 41.2
- Cholesterol: 0

## 34. Kalua Pua'a (Roast Pork)

*Serving: 1 pork butt, 4 serving(s) | Prep: 30mins | Ready in:*

### Ingredients

- 3 lbs pork butt
- 3 tablespoons hawaiian salt or 3 tablespoons sea salt
- ti leaves
- 1/2 gal. water

### Direction

- Rinse pork with cold water and place in a medium roasting pan. Rub Hawaiian salt on pork and add water. Cover pork with ti leaves and cover roasting pan with foil. Bake at 350* for 2-3 hours, or until meat is soft. Remove foil and ti leaves, debone and shred pork; add more salt if needed for taste.

### Nutrition Information

- Calories: 755.2
- Total Fat: 53.4
- Saturated Fat: 18.5
- Cholesterol: 224.5
- Sodium: 5439.9
- Fiber: 0
- Sugar: 0
- Total Carbohydrate: 0
- Protein: 63.8

## 35. Kapisi Pulu (Cabbage Beef Brisket In Coconut Cream)

*Serving: 4 serving(s) | Prep: 10mins | Ready in:*

### Ingredients

- 8 -10 large cabbage leaves
- 1 lb corned beef or 1 lb beef brisket
- 1 onion, chopped
- 1 tomatoes, chopped
- thick coconut cream

### Direction

- Place about 6 cabbage leaves on foil to make a cup shape. (It would help to put all these in a round cake tin). Into the cup-shaped cabbage leaves, put the corned beef, onion, tomato, some shredded cabbage and coconut cream.
- Wrap the foil around and bake in a moderate oven for about 1 to 1 and half hours. (This is normally baked in the umu).
- Serving suggestions: kumala (sweet potato) goes well with this dish.
- NOTE: This is similar to the "lu pulu". Here, cabbage is used instead of the taro leaves and then the procedure is the same for both. In fact, this dish can utilise any large leafy vegetable, hence spinach is an excellent substitute. Where fresh coconut cream is scarce and expensive, fresh thickened cream is a successful substitute mixed with coconut cream in a tin. Coconut cream now comes in powdered packages so you can mix to your preferred creaminess.

### Nutrition Information

- Calories: 317.9
- Total Fat: 21.7
- Saturated Fat: 7.2
- Sugar: 4.1
- Total Carbohydrate: 8.1
- Cholesterol: 111.2
- Protein: 22
- Sodium: 1301.6

- Fiber: 2.5

## 36. Kauai Pepita Pate

*Serving: 3 cups, about | Prep: 15mins | Ready in:*

### Ingredients

- 2 cups raw pumpkin seeds, soaked in distilled water for 1-2 hours (pepita)
- 1 jalapeno, seeded
- 1/4 cup olive oil
- 2 limes, juice of
- 1 teaspoon salt
- 1 teaspoon cumin
- 1 bunch cilantro, washed and minced
- 1/4 cup scallion, whites thinly sliced
- 1/2 cup tomatoes, seeded and chopped (1/8-inch pieces)

### Direction

- Grind pepita, jalapeno, oil, lime juice, and seasonings in food processor.
- Add water as needed, about 1/2 cup.
- When it's smooth, remove from processor.
- Fold in cilantro, scallions and tomato.
- Enjoy with crackers, as a dip, spread, or a tasty filling.

### Nutrition Information

- Calories: 667.6
- Saturated Fat: 10
- Sodium: 791.2
- Cholesterol: 0
- Total Fat: 60.6
- Fiber: 7.5
- Sugar: 3.2
- Total Carbohydrate: 16.7
- Protein: 27.1

## 37. Kokoda (Fijian Spicy Fish)

*Serving: 6-8 serving(s) | Prep: 30mins | Ready in:*

### Ingredients

- 4 large white fish fillets, such as mahi-mahi
- 3 large limes, juiced
- 1/2 teaspoon salt
- 1 cup coconut cream
- 1 large onion, minced
- 1 small green chili pepper, such as serrano, seeds and stem removed, minced
- 2 medium tomatoes, diced
- 1 bell pepper, seeds and stem removed, diced

### Direction

- Cut the fish into bite-size pieces. In a non-reactive bowl, combine the fish, lime juice, and salt. Marinate overnight in the refrigerator.
- Remove from the refrigerator, add the coconut cream, chopped onion, and chile just before serving. Sprinkle the tomatoes and bell pepper over the top. Serve on a bed of lettuce in coconut bilos (half coconut shells).
- Heat Scale: Mild.

### Nutrition Information

- Calories: 265.7
- Total Carbohydrate: 35.3
- Cholesterol: 41.1
- Protein: 13
- Total Fat: 9.1
- Saturated Fat: 7.8
- Sodium: 260.6
- Fiber: 2.4
- Sugar: 29

## 38. Kona Coffee Barbeuce Sauce

*Serving: 2 cups | Prep: 20mins | Ready in:*

## Ingredients

- 2 tablespoons roasted garlic
- 1 onion, yellow, diced and caramelized
- 1 cup brown sugar, packed
- 2 cups coffee, strong Kona coffee
- 1 cup cider vinegar
- 2 cups ketchup
- 1 cup Worcestershire sauce
- 1 tablespoon celery salt
- 2 tablespoons dried chipotle powder
- 2 tablespoons Dijon mustard
- 1/2 cup honey

## Direction

- Combine all ingredients in saucepan and bring to boil.
- Reduce heat to simmer, and reduce by 1/2.
- Using stick blender, blend until smooth.
- Cool and use as needed.

## Nutrition Information

- Calories: 1110.3
- Sodium: 4371.1
- Total Carbohydrate: 278.6
- Cholesterol: 0
- Saturated Fat: 0.4
- Fiber: 5.3
- Sugar: 248.4
- Protein: 7.7
- Total Fat: 2.6

## 39. Lomi Lomi Salmon

*Serving: 2 serving(s) | Prep: 15mins | Ready in:*

## Ingredients

- 4 ounces smoked salmon, chopped
- 1/2 cup green onion, sliced
- 1/2 cup tomatoes, peeled, chopped
- 2 tablespoons green peppers, chopped

## Direction

- Mix all ingredients together with hands.
- Chill well before serving.

## Nutrition Information

- Calories: 88.4
- Sodium: 477.8
- Sugar: 2
- Total Carbohydrate: 4.1
- Total Fat: 2.8
- Cholesterol: 13.8
- Protein: 11.9
- Saturated Fat: 0.6
- Fiber: 1.4

## 40. Mangoes Foster With Creme Fraiche (By Bobby Flay)

*Serving: 6 mango halves, 6 serving(s) | Prep: 5mins | Ready in:*

## Ingredients

- 3 slightly under-ripe mangoes
- 1/2 cup unsalted butter (1 stick)
- 1/2 cup packed light brown sugar
- 1/3 cup Bourbon
- 1/4 teaspoon ground cinnamon
- 1/8 teaspoon salt
- 1/2 cup chopped toasted pecans
- 1/2 cup creme fraiche (optional) or 1/2 cup sour cream (optional)

## Direction

- Heat the grill to high.
- Halve each mango and remove the pits. (To make it easier, I have cut the mangoes in quarters because it makes it easier to cut them away from the pit.) Remove the peels from each mango half. Cut diamond shapes about

1/2-inch deep in the top of the mango flesh, but be careful to not cut all the way through.

- Place a medium saucepan on the grates of the grill (or on stove top over medium heat). Add the butter and brown sugar to the pan. Cook, stirring occasionally until the sugar has melted and the sauce thickens slightly, about 5 minutes.
- Remove the pan from the heat and add the bourbon. Using a long match, ignite the bourbon and allow the flames to subside. Stir in the cinnamon, salt and chopped pecans.
- Top mangoes with the sauce and garnish with a dollop of crème fraiche or sour cream, if using. (I usually skip the sour cream and just sprinkle a little extra chopped pecans).

## Nutrition Information

- Calories: 371.4
- Protein: 1.5
- Total Fat: 22.2
- Saturated Fat: 10.3
- Sodium: 59.9
- Total Carbohydrate: 36.8
- Fiber: 2.8
- Sugar: 33.3
- Cholesterol: 40.7

## 41. Maui Wowie Shrimp Salad

*Serving: 4 serving(s) | Prep: 25mins | Ready in:*

## Ingredients

- Dressing
- 2 teaspoons minced shallots
- 1 teaspoon capers
- 1/4 cup fresh lime juice
- 1/2 cup plus 1 tablespoon olive oil
- 3/4 teaspoon Dijon mustard
- 1 tablespoon honey
- The Rest

- 4 vine ripened tomatoes, sliced very thin (about 1 pound)
- 1/3 cup crumbled feta cheese
- 2 tablespoons capers
- 1/3 cup finely chopped sweet onion
- 12 large cooked shrimp, each cut crosswise into 3 pieces (grilled shrimp works great)
- 1/2 medium avocado, diced into pieces the same size as the shrimp
- 8 bibb lettuce, cut into 1/8 inch strips
- 4 popcorn shoot mixed sprouts (optional)

## Direction

- DRESSING PREPARATION: Combine shallots, 1 teaspoon capers and lime juice in a blender and purée until smooth. Add olive oil and mustard and blend until well combined. Stir in honey.
- TO ARRANGE SALAD: Arrange 5 slices of tomato on each of four plates, overlapping them to form a circle with a hole in the middle.
- Combine feta, 2 tablespoons capers and onion, drizzle with some dressing and salt and pepper to taste and toss well.
- Combine shrimp and avocado in another bowl, drizzle with some dressing and salt and pepper to taste and toss well. Drizzle lettuce with a little dressing and salt and pepper to taste and toss well.
- Mound 1/4 of the lettuce in center of tomato ring. Spoon one 1/4 of the feta and shrimp mixture on top. Drizzle tomatoes and salad with some of the remaining dressing. Garnish with popcorn shoot sprouts, if desired.

## Nutrition Information

- Calories: 424.1
- Total Fat: 34.7
- Saturated Fat: 6.3
- Sugar: 12.1
- Total Carbohydrate: 22.4
- Protein: 11.9
- Sodium: 480.7
- Fiber: 7.2

- Cholesterol: 45.9

## 42. Menehune Juice

*Serving: 1 cocktails, 1 serving(s) | Prep: 2mins | Ready in:*

## Ingredients

- 2 ounces bacardi superior rum
- 1/2 ounce Cointreau liqueur
- 1/4 ounce almond syrup (Also known as orgeat, Try almond from DaVinci or Monin)
- 3/4 ounce freshly squeezed lime juice
- 1/4 ounce simple syrup
- Garnish
- lime wedge and mint

## Direction

- Shake all ingredients with ice and strain into an old fashioned glass filled with crushed ice.
- Garnish with lime and mint.

## Nutrition Information

- Calories: 133.8
- Sodium: 1
- Total Carbohydrate: 1.8
- Protein: 0.1
- Cholesterol: 0
- Total Fat: 0
- Saturated Fat: 0
- Fiber: 0.1
- Sugar: 0.4

## 43. Molokai Venison Stew

*Serving: 6 serving(s) | Prep: 5mins | Ready in:*

## Ingredients

- 1/2 cup wine vinegar
- 2 cups plum wine
- 1 cup finely chopped onion
- 3 garlic cloves, finely chopped
- salt and pepper
- 1 bay leaf
- 1/4 teaspoon oregano
- 1/4 teaspoon thyme
- 3 -4 lbs lean venison, cut into 1-inch cubes
- 2 -3 tablespoons oil
- 2 cups canned whole tomatoes

## Direction

- Combine vinegar, plum wine, onions, garlic, salt, pepper, bay leaf, oregano and time in a non-reactive bowl and mix well.
- Add venison and toss to coat.
- Cover and refrigerate several hours or overnight, stirring occasionally.
- Drain and reserve marinade.
- Heat oil in a heavy pot or Dutch oven.
- Add meat and brown well on all sides.
- Add marinade and tomatoes.
- Cover and simmer over low heat until meat is tender, about 1 1/2-2 hours.

## Nutrition Information

- Calories: 335.3
- Saturated Fat: 2.7
- Fiber: 1.3
- Sugar: 3
- Cholesterol: 190.4
- Protein: 52.4
- Total Fat: 10.1
- Sodium: 207.5
- Total Carbohydrate: 6.2

## 44. Moorea Nui

*Serving: 20 glasses | Prep: 20mins | Ready in:*

## Ingredients

- 2 cups white rum
- 2 cups dark rum
- 2/3 cup white Curacao
- 6 cups orange juice
- 6 cups pineapple juice
- 2/3 cup simple syrup
- 1 vanilla bean
- 1 lime
- 1 lemon

## Direction

- Mix together the rums, white Curacao, fruit juices and simple syrup.
- Split the vanilla bean down the middle and scoop out the seeds. Add these to the mixture along with the bean.
- Wash the lime and lemon thoroughly. Cut the lemon into quarters and add to the punch. Juice the lime and add to the punch. Mix well.
- Chill the punch for 6 hours to allow the flavors to blend.

## Nutrition Information

- Calories: 177.8
- Saturated Fat: 0
- Cholesterol: 0
- Protein: 0.8
- Total Fat: 0.2
- Sodium: 2.8
- Fiber: 0.5
- Sugar: 13.9
- Total Carbohydrate: 18

## 45. Nuku Hiva Nui

*Serving: 20 glasses | Prep: 20mins | Ready in:*

## Ingredients

- 2 cups white rum
- 2 cups dark rum
- 2/3 cup Grand Marnier
- 6 cups orange juice
- 6 cups pineapple juice
- 2 cups carbonated lemon-lime beverage
- 1 vanilla bean
- 1 cinnamon stick
- 2 oranges, unwaxed washed well finely sliced

## Direction

- Mix together the rums, Grand Marnier, fruit juices and lemon-lime soda.
- Split the vanilla bean down the middle and scoop out the seeds. Add these to the mixture along with the bean.
- Add cinnamon stick and orange slices to the punch.
- Chill the punch for 6 hours to allow the flavors to blend. Most of the carbonation from the soda will have evaporated. This is ok.

## Nutrition Information

- Calories: 192
- Total Fat: 0.3
- Fiber: 0.6
- Sugar: 17.2
- Total Carbohydrate: 21.4
- Cholesterol: 0
- Saturated Fat: 0
- Sodium: 4.9
- Protein: 0.9

## 46. Overnight Pupu Spareribs

*Serving: 10 serving(s) | Prep: 24hours | Ready in:*

## Ingredients

- 5 lbs spareribs
- 4 cloves garlic, crushed
- 1 piece gingerroot, crushed
- 1 teaspoon salt
- 1 cup brown sugar
- 1 cup soy sauce

- 1 cup ketchup
- 1/3 cup oyster sauce

## Direction

- Cut spareribs into 1 1/2 inch pieces.
- Combine ribs, garlic, ginger, and salt in a large pot with lid.
- Add water to cover ribs, bring to a boil, lower heat to minimum, cover and simmer until ribs are tender (approx. 1 to 1 1/2 hours).
- Drain.
- Mix the remaining ingredients and coat ribs well.
- Marinate overnight in the refrigerator.
- Broil ribs 3 inches from element for 7-10 minutes, basting with remaining sauce.
- Turn and broil for 5-7 more minutes.
- If preferred the barbeque can be used instead of the broiler.

## Nutrition Information

- Calories: 1030.1
- Cholesterol: 274.3
- Protein: 69.5
- Saturated Fat: 25.2
- Fiber: 0.4
- Sugar: 27.1
- Total Fat: 68.8
- Sodium: 2595.6
- Total Carbohydrate: 30.5

## 47. Pai Ika/ Cook Islands Fish Fingers

*Serving: 2-4 serving(s) | Prep: 15mins | Ready in:*

## Ingredients

- 2 cups cooked fish, cold
- 1 cup sweet potatoes or 1 cup kumara, cold and mashed
- 1 egg

- 1 cup of left over vegetables, chopped finely
- salt and pepper
- breadcrumbs

## Direction

- Combine everything in a bowl and mash well with a fork.
- Take spoonfuls of the mixture and roll into finger shapes.
- Roll in breadcrumbs.
- Fry in a little oil until golden brown.
- Remove from pan and set aside to cool.
- Store in the fridge.

## Nutrition Information

- Calories: 93.9
- Fiber: 2
- Sugar: 3
- Cholesterol: 105.8
- Protein: 4.2
- Total Fat: 2.5
- Total Carbohydrate: 13.6
- Saturated Fat: 0.8
- Sodium: 71.6

## 48. Papaya And Strawberry Coulis Over Pound Cake

*Serving: 6 serving(s) | Prep: 10mins | Ready in:*

## Ingredients

- 10 3/4 ounces frozen pound cake
- 1 cup individually frozen strawberries
- 1/4 cup rum (light or dark) or 1/4 cup unsweetened apple juice
- 3/4 cup chopped papaya
- whipped cream

## Direction

- Cut pound cake into 6 slices and arrange on individual serving plates.

- Combine the strawberries and rum (juice) in blender. Cover and pulse on and off until the mixture becomes a coarse puree.
- Add papaya to blender and pulse until the mixture is smooth.
- Pour 1/4 cup coulis (puree) over each cake slice and top with a dollop of whip cream.
- Serve at once.

## Nutrition Information

- Calories: 240.5
- Total Fat: 9.2
- Sodium: 206.1
- Sugar: 2.7
- Total Carbohydrate: 31.9
- Cholesterol: 29.7
- Saturated Fat: 2.4
- Fiber: 1.6
- Protein: 2.9

## 49. Passionfruit Applesauce

*Serving: 5 c | Prep: 10mins | Ready in:*

### Ingredients

- 3 lbs apples, peeled, cored and quartered (your choice of variety)
- 1/3 cup passion fruit juice, strained (or nectar)
- 1/2 vanilla bean, split
- 2 slices ginger, 1/4-inch, gently crushed
- 1/2 cup mirin
- 3 tablespoons honey (or to taste)

### Direction

- Place all ingredients in a heavy non-reactive saucepan over medium heat.
- Cover and cook until apples are very soft, 10-15 minutes. Reduce temperature if apples start to boil over.
- Remove from heat and take out ginger and vanilla bean.

- Place apple mixture in food processor and puree into a smooth sauce.

## Nutrition Information

- Calories: 249
- Sodium: 149.6
- Sugar: 50.5
- Total Carbohydrate: 64.7
- Protein: 1.1
- Total Fat: 0.7
- Saturated Fat: 0.1
- Fiber: 9.2
- Cholesterol: 0

## 50. Pina Colada Martini

*Serving: 1 drink, 1 serving(s) | Prep: 3mins | Ready in:*

### Ingredients

- 1/2 ounce blue curacao
- 1 1/2 ounces pineapple juice
- 1 ounce vanilla vodka
- 1 ounce coconut rum (Malibu)

### Direction

- In a shaker with ice combine all ingredients. Shake and strain into four ounce martini glass.

## Nutrition Information

- Calories: 317.9
- Saturated Fat: 0
- Fiber: 0.1
- Cholesterol: 0
- Total Fat: 0.1
- Total Carbohydrate: 5.5
- Protein: 0.1
- Sodium: 2.1
- Sugar: 4.3

## 51. Po'e (Tahitian Fruit Pudding)

*Serving: 4-6 serving(s) | Prep: 15mins | Ready in:*

### Ingredients

- 6 -8 ripe bananas, peeled and cut into chunks
- 1/2 cup brown sugar
- 1 cup arrowroot or 1 cup cornstarch
- 2 teaspoons vanilla
- 1 cup coconut cream

### Direction

- Preheat oven to 375°F.
- Puree the bananas in a blender or food processor. It should yield 4 cups.
- Mix the brown sugar and arrowroot or cornstarch together. Add in the vanilla and combine with the bananas and process well. There should not be any lumps of starch. Adjust the sugar to your liking.
- Pour the mix in a buttered 2-quart baking dish.
- Bake for 30-45 minutes, or until the pudding is firm and bubbling.
- Remove from oven and allow to cool. Cover with plastic wrap and refrigerate until well chilled.
- Once chilled, cut into cubes and place them into a large serving bowl or in individual bowls.
- Top with a dollop of coconut cream and a little more brown sugar and serve.

### Nutrition Information

- Calories: 523.6
- Sugar: 52.9
- Total Carbohydrate: 101.8
- Protein: 4
- Total Fat: 13.7
- Sodium: 50.3
- Saturated Fat: 11.8
- Fiber: 7.3
- Cholesterol: 0

## 52. Polynesian Crock Pot Spareribs

*Serving: 4 serving(s) | Prep: 5mins | Ready in:*

### Ingredients

- 3 -4 lbs pork spareribs
- 5 tablespoons sugar
- 3 tablespoons honey
- 3 tablespoons soy sauce
- 2 tablespoons ketchup
- 1 teaspoon seasoning salt
- 1 cup chicken broth

### Direction

- Place ribs in the bottom of your slow cooker.
- Mix remaining ingredients and pour over ribs.
- Cover and cook on low for 8- 9 hours.
- *If the ribs are fatty boil for 5 minutes before placing in slow cooker.

### Nutrition Information

- Calories: 1106.6
- Saturated Fat: 30.5
- Sugar: 30.8
- Total Carbohydrate: 31.6
- Cholesterol: 265.4
- Total Fat: 80.7
- Protein: 61
- Sodium: 1286
- Fiber: 0.2

## 53. Polynesian Flank Steak

*Serving: 6 serving(s) | Prep: 15mins | Ready in:*

### Ingredients

- 1/3 cup pineapple juice

- 1/3 cup low sodium soy sauce
- 1/4 cup green onion, thinly sliced
- 1 tablespoon fresh ginger, minced peeled
- 1 tablespoon honey
- 1 garlic clove, minced
- 1 1/2 lbs flank steaks
- cooking spray

## Direction

- Combine first 6 ingredients in a large zip-top bag; add steak to bag.  Seal and marinate in refrigerator 3 hours, turning once.
- Prepare grill.
- Remove steak from bag, reserving marinade. Place steak on grill rack coated with cooking spray; grill 20 minutes or until desired degree of doneness, turning and basting frequently with the reserved marinade.  Let stand 10 minutes before cutting diagonally across the grain into thin slices.

## Nutrition Information

- Calories: 215.5
- Sodium: 534.2
- Fiber: 0.3
- Sugar: 4.6
- Total Carbohydrate: 6.5
- Cholesterol: 46.5
- Protein: 25
- Total Fat: 9.4
- Saturated Fat: 3.9

## 54. Polynesian Ham Sauce

*Serving: 6 serving(s) | Prep: 5mins | Ready in:*

## Ingredients

- 1 (15 ounce) can peach slices, drained and chopped
- 1 cup crushed pineapple, drained
- 2 tablespoons cornstarch

- 1/2 teaspoon cinnamon
- 1 pinch clove
- 1/3 cup frozen orange juice concentrate, slighty thawed
- 1 cup water
- 1/3 cup raisins
- 1/2 cup maraschino cherry, left whole or sliced in half (optional)

## Direction

- In a saucepan combine the cornstarch with cinnamon and cloves; add in the reserved peach and pineapple juice, orange juice concentrate and water.
- Bring to a boil and simmer over medium heat until thickened and bubbly.
- Reduce heat, then stir in chopped peaches, crushed pineapple, raisins and cherries (if using) simmer 1-2 minutes.
- Serve this warm or cooled with ham.

## Nutrition Information

- Calories: 85.8
- Saturated Fat: 0
- Sodium: 3
- Sugar: 16.9
- Total Carbohydrate: 21.8
- Protein: 0.8
- Total Fat: 0.1
- Fiber: 0.9
- Cholesterol: 0

## 55. Polynesian Inspired Vegetarian Pilau

*Serving: 6 serving(s) | Prep: 45mins | Ready in:*

## Ingredients

- 16 ounces black-eyed peas, drained
- 2 cups brown rice, cooked
- 4 tablespoons butter

- 1 cup peanuts, chopped
- 1 large onion, chopped
- 1 tablespoon fresh ginger, grated
- 1 large green pepper, diced
- 4 cups celery, chopped
- 1 carrot, sliced thin
- 1 cup green peas
- 1 cup pineapple tidbits, reserve 2Tbl . juice
- 2 tablespoons soy sauce
- 1 dash salt
- 1 dash hot pepper sauce

## Direction

- In a large pan, sauté peanuts in 1 Tbl. butter until toasty. Take out the peanuts and set them aside.
- To the butter in the pan add the grated ginger, the onion, along with another 1 Tbl. butter. Cook until the onions are translucent.
- Add the remaining butter, the chopped celery, carrot, and the diced green pepper. Cook until slightly tender.
- Add the rest of the ingredients, except for the rice. Bring just to a boil and then take off the heat.
- Stir in the cooked rice. Sprinkle toasted peanuts on top.

## Nutrition Information

- Calories: 557.7
- Cholesterol: 20.4
- Sodium: 715.6
- Sugar: 8.7
- Total Carbohydrate: 75.8
- Protein: 18
- Total Fat: 22.2
- Saturated Fat: 7.1
- Fiber: 10.6

## 56. Polynesian Pineapple Shake

*Serving: 4 serving(s) | Prep: 10mins | Ready in:*

## Ingredients

- 2 1/4 cups ginger ale, chilled
- 2 cups pineapple sherbet, softened
- 2 tablespoons fresh lime juice
- lime slice, garnish

## Direction

- Combine the first 3 ingredients in blender, and blend until creamy.

## Nutrition Information

- Calories: 48.5
- Total Carbohydrate: 12.7
- Sodium: 9.8
- Fiber: 0
- Sugar: 12.1
- Cholesterol: 0
- Protein: 0
- Total Fat: 0
- Saturated Fat: 0

## 57. Polynesian Pork Roast

*Serving: 12 serving(s) | Prep: 10mins | Ready in:*

## Ingredients

- 4 lbs pork roast
- 3⁄4 cup pineapple apricot jam
- 1/2 cup brown sugar
- 1 teaspoon minced garlic
- 1⁄4 cup apple cider vinegar
- 1/2 cup soy sauce
- 1⁄4 cup molasses
- 2 cups chicken broth

## Direction

- Place pork roast in slow cooker. Combine jam, brown sugar, garlic, vinegar, soy sauce, molasses and chicken broth. Mix well.

- Pour over roast. Cover and cook on low for 8 hours.
- Remove roast and sauce from slow cooker. Allow to cool.
- Place cooled roast and sauce in freezer bag. Label and freeze.
- To serve: thaw. Heat roast and sauce until hot and bubbly. Pull roast into serving pieces (or shred) and serve sauce over rice.

## Nutrition Information

- Calories: 310.7
- Sodium: 895.9
- Sugar: 21.8
- Cholesterol: 104.3
- Protein: 35.5
- Saturated Fat: 1.7
- Fiber: 0.2
- Total Carbohydrate: 28.1
- Total Fat: 5.9

## 58. Polynesian Pork And Rice

*Serving: 4-6 serving(s) | Prep: 20mins | Ready in:*

## Ingredients

- 1 1/2-2 lbs pork butt (or shoulder, or pork steak)
- 1/4 cup flour
- 1 1/2 teaspoons salt
- 1/8 teaspoon pepper
- 2 tablespoons extra virgin olive oil (or canola oil)
- 1 cup celery
- 1 medium green pepper
- 1 small onion
- 1 (15 ounce) can pineapple tidbits (or chunks, drained)
- 1/3 cup ketchup
- 2 teaspoons prepared mustard
- 1 teaspoon Worcestershire sauce
- 3/4-1 cup juice (from the canned fruit or fruit juice)
- 4 cups cooked rice

## Direction

- Cut the pork in 1-inch cubes.
- Mix the flour, salt and pepper.
- Coat the pork with the flour mixture using all the flour.
- Brown in oil in a large pan.
- Slice the celery and onion.
- Slice the peppers into thin strips.
- Add the vegetables to the pan along with the remaining ingredients. (**Do not add rice).
- Simmer covered for 30 minutes.
- Serve over rice.
- Enjoy!

## Nutrition Information

- Calories: 800
- Fiber: 3.6
- Cholesterol: 112.3
- Total Fat: 34.3
- Sugar: 17.1
- Total Carbohydrate: 82.3
- Protein: 38.8
- Saturated Fat: 10.4
- Sodium: 1263.8

## 59. Polynesian Potato Brunch Scramble #5FIX

*Serving: 4-6 serving(s) | Prep: 10mins | Ready in:*

## Ingredients

- 6 ounces thick-cut lean pepper bacon, chopped
- 1 medium sweet red pepper, diced
- 1 (20 ounce) package Simply Potatoes Diced Potatoes with Onion
- 2 cups drained pineapple tidbits

- 8 ounces shredded medium-sharp cheddar cheese

## Direction

- In large skillet, over medium heat, cook bacon and pepper about 3 minutes.
- Add potatoes with onions and cook over medium heat, covered for about 20 minutes, turning with a spatula every 3-4 minutes.
- Gently stir in the pineapple and half the cheese. Sprinkle remaining cheese on top and reduce heat to simmer.
- Cover and simmer about 6 minutes.

## Nutrition Information

- Calories: 474.1
- Cholesterol: 88.6
- Protein: 19.8
- Sodium: 709
- Fiber: 1.8
- Total Carbohydrate: 13.6
- Total Fat: 38.2
- Saturated Fat: 18.4
- Sugar: 9.7

## 60. Polynesian Rice

*Serving: 6 serving(s) | Prep: 5mins | Ready in:*

## Ingredients

- 2 cups uncooked rice
- 3 3/4 cups chicken broth
- 2 teaspoons soy sauce
- 1 (8 ounce) can crushed pineapple (with juice)
- 2 tablespoons butter
- 1 tablespoon diced onion
- 1 tablespoon diced bell pepper
- 1 garlic clove, minced

## Direction

- Combine all ingredients in rice cooker.

- Cook 20 minutes, or until rice is done.
- Fluff with a fork before serving.

## Nutrition Information

- Calories: 316.9
- Protein: 7.8
- Sodium: 617.1
- Sugar: 6
- Saturated Fat: 2.8
- Fiber: 1.3
- Total Carbohydrate: 58.4
- Cholesterol: 10.2
- Total Fat: 5.1

## 61. Polynesian Shrimp Florida Style

*Serving: 6 serving(s) | Prep: 10mins | Ready in:*

## Ingredients

- 1 lb shrimp, cooked, peeled and deveined
- 1 cup fresh pineapple chunk
- 1 cup celery, thinly sliced
- 1/2 cup green seedless grape
- 1/4 cup green onion, sliced
- 2 tablespoons mayonnaise
- 2 tablespoons sour cream
- 1/2 teaspoon salt
- 1/8 teaspoon white pepper
- salad greens
- paprika

## Direction

- Cut any large shrimp in half.
- Drain pineapple, reserving 2 tbsp of the juice.
- Combine shrimp, pineapple, celery, grapes and green onions in 2 quart bowl.
- Combine pineapple juice, mayonnaise, sour cream, salt and pepper, mix well.
- Pour over shrimp mixture and toss lightly. Chill at least 30 minutes.
- Serve on salad greens.

- Sprinkle with paprika.

## Nutrition Information

- Calories: 127.9
- Sugar: 5.2
- Total Carbohydrate: 7.9
- Protein: 16.4
- Total Fat: 3.4
- Saturated Fat: 1
- Fiber: 0.9
- Sodium: 414.6
- Cholesterol: 150.3

## 62. Polynesian Wedding Cake

*Serving: 1 cake, 6-8 serving(s) | Prep: 20mins | Ready in:*

### Ingredients

- 2 cups flour
- 2 teaspoons cinnamon
- 2 teaspoons baking soda
- 1 teaspoon salt
- 1 (8 ounce) can crushed pineapple, drained
- 1 1/4 cups vegetable oil
- 3 eggs
- 2 cups sugar
- 2 cups finely shredded carrots
- 1 cup chopped nuts
- 3/4 cup shredded coconut
- 1 cup chopped dates (optional) or 1 cup raisins (optional)
- cream cheese frosting
- 1 (3 ounce) package cream cheese, softened
- 1 tablespoon milk
- 1/2 teaspoon vanilla
- 1/4 cup butter, softened
- 1 cup toasted coconut
- 3 cups confectioners' sugar

### Direction

- Preheat oven to 350°F.
- Grease a 13-by-9-inch baking pan and set aside.
- In a large mixing bowl, using a wooden spoon (do not use a mixer), combine oil and sugar until blended.
- Add eggs, one at a time, mixing well after each addition, and vanilla. Gradually add dry ingredients, stirring until well blended.
- Add shredded carrots, chopped nuts, pineapple and coconut and mix just until combined.
- Bake for 50 minutes or until top of cake springs back when lightly touched.
- After cake has cooled, top with cream cheese frosting or serve plain.
- Cream Cheese Frosting:
- Cream together the cream cheese and butter.
- Add confectioners' sugar, milk, vanilla and most of the toasted coconut. Let cake cool completely and spread frosting on top. Decorate top with toasted coconut, if desired. Variation: Substituting 1 teaspoon of lemon zest for the vanilla and 1/2 teaspoon of fresh lemon juice for the milk will produce a nice lemony frosting.

## Nutrition Information

- Calories: 1529.2
- Sodium: 1178.1
- Saturated Fat: 27.8
- Sugar: 140.6
- Total Carbohydrate: 184.7
- Cholesterol: 129.3
- Protein: 14.3
- Total Fat: 86
- Fiber: 8

## 63. Polynesian Meatballs

*Serving: 4-6 serving(s) | Prep: 10mins | Ready in:*

### Ingredients

- Meatballs
- 1 lb lean hamburger
- 1/2 cup dry breadcrumbs
- 1 teaspoon basil
- 1 teaspoon pepper
- 1/2 teaspoon salt
- 1/4 cup dried onion flakes
- Sauce
- 1 (10 ounce) can tomato soup
- 1 (14 ounce) can pineapple tidbits, drained
- 1/3 cup brown sugar
- 1/2 green peppers or 1/2 red pepper, chopped

## Direction

- For the meatballs, mix all the ingredients together and roll into small balls.
- Brown the meatballs in a non-stick frying pan.
- Combine all the ingredients for the sauce in a casserole dish, mixing in the meatballs after they are browned.
- Bake the meatballs and sauce, covered, at 350 degrees for 25 minutes, until bubbling.
- Serve over rice.

## Nutrition Information

- Calories: 273.5
- Total Fat: 3.8
- Saturated Fat: 1.4
- Sugar: 35.1
- Protein: 9
- Sodium: 806.4
- Fiber: 3.6
- Total Carbohydrate: 53.6
- Cholesterol: 16.2

## 64. Potluck Polynesian Chicken Recipe

*Serving: 8 serving(s) | Prep: 30mins | Ready in:*

## Ingredients

- 1 cup buttermilk
- 1 cup all-purpose flour
- 1 teaspoon salt
- 1/4 teaspoon black pepper
- 3 -4 lbs chicken pieces (we use boneless chicken tenders boneless thighs)
- 1 cup peanut oil
- 1 (20 ounce) can pineapple chunks in juice
- 1/2 cup sugar
- 2 tablespoons cornstarch
- 1/2 cup cider vinegar
- 1 tablespoon reduced sodium soy sauce
- 1/4 teaspoon ground ginger
- 1 medium green bell pepper, sliced into thin strips
- cooked rice (optional)

## Direction

- Preheat oven to 350 degrees. Grease a 13 x 9-inch baking pan.
- Pour buttermilk into a shallow bowl. Combine flour, salt and pepper in a separate shallow bowl.
- Dip chicken in buttermilk and dredge in flour mixture.
- Heat oil in a large skillet over medium-high heat. Add chicken and cook until browned; transfer to baking pan.
- Drain pineapple, reserving juice. Add enough water to equal 1½ cups liquid.
- Combine sugar and cornstarch in a medium saucepan. Add pineapple liquid, vinegar, soy sauce and ginger.
- Stir until cornstarch is completely dissolved. Bring to a boil and cook 2 minutes, stirring constantly. Pour over chicken.
- Bake, uncovered, 30 minutes. Add pineapple and green pepper strips. Bake 15 minutes longer, or until chicken is tender and no longer pink in the center.
- Serve over rice, if using.

## Nutrition Information

- Calories: 636.5

- Fiber: 1.3
- Sugar: 24.7
- Protein: 22.4
- Total Carbohydrate: 39.9
- Cholesterol: 78.8
- Total Fat: 43.1
- Saturated Fat: 9.2
- Sodium: 472.7

## 65. Ranch Coconut Lemon Shrimp #RSC

*Serving: 4-6 serving(s) | Prep: 5mins | Ready in:*

### Ingredients

- 1 1/2 lbs shrimp, peeled and deveined
- 1 (4 ounce) package Hidden Valley Original Ranch Seasoning Mix
- 8 ounces Greek yogurt
- 1/2 cup cream of coconut
- 2 lemons, juice and zest of
- 1/2 cup parmesan cheese, freshly grated
- 1/2 cup shredded coconut

### Direction

- In a large skillet over medium-high heat, stir all ingredients (yes, it's that easy) until shrimp is no longer pink. Serve. This is great over rice or pasta.

### Nutrition Information

- Calories: 370.3
- Cholesterol: 225.3
- Fiber: 0.7
- Sodium: 1197.9
- Sugar: 24.8
- Total Carbohydrate: 28.9
- Protein: 28.8
- Total Fat: 15.5
- Saturated Fat: 11.8

## 66. Shrimp W/ Mango Rice

*Serving: 6 serving(s) | Prep: 1hours | Ready in:*

### Ingredients

- 1 tablespoon fresh garlic, minced
- 1 tablespoon fresh ginger, peeled minced
- 1 tablespoon soy sauce
- 4 teaspoons curry powder
- 1/8 teaspoon ground red pepper
- 1/8 teaspoon ground cumin
- 1 1/2 lbs medium shrimp, peeled devined
- 2 cups water
- 1 cup coconut milk
- 1 1/4 cups wild rice, uncooked (brown rice optional)
- 3/4 cup carrot, shredded
- 2 mangoes, peeled diced
- 1 1/2 cups red peppers, diced
- 1/2 cup green onion, chopped
- 1 tablespoon fresh cilantro, chopped
- 1 tablespoon fresh parsley, chopped
- 2 tablespoons lime juice
- 1/2 teaspoon salt

### Direction

- Combine the first 6 ingredients in a medium bowl, add shrimp, toss to coat, cover chill 1 hours.
- Bring water and coconut milk to a boil in a medium saucepan. Add rice cover. Reduce heat simmer 30 minutes or until liquid is absorbed.
- Remove from heat add next 8 ingredients; toss gently to combine.
- Prepare sauté pan to medium heat and coat with cooking spray.
- Place shrimp in pan cook 3 minutes on each side, until pink/done.
- Mix rice shrimp.
- Plate garnish.

### Nutrition Information

- Calories: 408.1
- Fiber: 6.3
- Sugar: 16.7
- Total Carbohydrate: 48.2
- Protein: 31
- Total Fat: 11.6
- Saturated Fat: 8.3
- Sodium: 572.9
- Cholesterol: 172.8

## 67. Slaw From Samoa

*Serving: 4 serving(s) | Prep: 10mins | Ready in:*

## Ingredients

- Slaw
- 4 cups cabbage, shredded
- 8 stuffed olives, sliced
- 1/4 bunch watercress
- 1 tablespoon chopped pimiento
- 1/4 cup chopped green pepper
- Dressing
- 1 teaspoon salt
- 1/4 teaspoon pepper
- 1/2 teaspoon dry mustard
- 1 tablespoon celery seed
- 2 tablespoons sugar
- 3 tablespoons salad oil
- 1/2 cup vinegar

## Direction

- Combine slaw ingredients in a large bowl.
- Cover and chill.
- Place dressing ingredients in a jar.
- Cover.
- When ready to serve, shake jar well to combine ingredients.
- Pour dressing over slaw and toss to mix.

## Nutrition Information

- Calories: 147.2

- Total Fat: 10.7
- Saturated Fat: 1.5
- Sodium: 628.4
- Sugar: 8.8
- Total Carbohydrate: 11.7
- Fiber: 2.2
- Cholesterol: 0
- Protein: 1.4

## 68. South Pacific Chicken Strips With Guava Dipping Sauce

*Serving: 6 serving(s) | Prep: 20mins | Ready in:*

## Ingredients

- SOUTH PACIFIC CHICKEN
- 1/2 cup pineapple juice
- 1/2 cup passion fruit nectar
- 2 tablespoons soy sauce
- 3 garlic cloves, minced
- 1 inch piece fresh ginger, minced
- 1/2 teaspoon ground allspice
- 1 teaspoon salt
- 1/2 teaspoon fresh ground black pepper
- 1 -2 pinch crushed red pepper flakes (optional)
- 1 1/2 lbs boneless skinless chicken breasts, cut in 1 1/2-inch long strips or 1 1/2 lbs chicken tenders
- GUAVA DIPPING SAUCE
- 1 cup guava nectar
- 1/4 cup pineapple juice
- 1/4 ounce dark rum (optional)
- 2 garlic cloves, minced
- 1 teaspoon fresh ginger, minced
- 1 pinch cinnamon
- 2 green onions, minced
- 3 tablespoons butter
- salt
- fresh ground black pepper
- green onion, finely minced, for garnish dipping sauce
- fresh pineapple, sliced, for garnish
- fresh kiwi, sliced, for garnish

## Direction

- Soak wooden skewers in water.
- Add pineapple juice, passion fruit nectar, soy sauce, garlic, ginger, allspice, salt, and pepper to a nonreactive baking dish large enough to hold all the chicken and mix well.
- Add chicken strips and turn to coat; cover and marinate for 30 minutes.
- Remove chicken from marinade, discarding marinade, and skewer each chicken strip.
- Thread chicken onto skewers and place skewers on a baking sheet.
- Broil in the oven about 6 inches from the heat for 7-8 minutes, turning once.
- GUAVA DIPPING SAUCE:
- Add guava nectar, pineapple juice, garlic, ginger, and green onions to a small saucepan over medium-high heat and reduce by half.
- Remove from heat and add butter, stirring until melted.
- Season to taste with salt and pepper and more green onions.
- TO SERVE:
- Place Guava Dipping Sauce in a small bowl, and place bowl in the middle of a large serving platter.
- Fan out South Pacific Chicken Skewers around bowl.
- Garnish platter with green onions and pineapple slices. .

## Nutrition Information

- Calories: 202.4
- Total Fat: 7.2
- Fiber: 0.4
- Sugar: 3.4
- Cholesterol: 81.1
- Protein: 27.3
- Saturated Fat: 4
- Sodium: 839.5
- Total Carbohydrate: 5.9

## 69. Spicy Apricot Sauce

*Serving: 1 1/2 cups, 6-8 serving(s) | Prep: 10mins | Ready in:*

## Ingredients

- 1 cup dried apricot
- 1 cup water
- 1/2 cup cider vinegar
- 1/4 cup sugar
- 2 tablespoons honey
- 1 teaspoon paprika
- 1/4 teaspoon salt

## Direction

- In a heavy 1- to 1 1/2- quart saucepan, combine the apricots and water and bring to a boil over high heat. Reduce the heat to the lowest possible point, cover tightly, and simmer for about 30 minutes, or until the apricots are soft and have absorbed almost all of the liquid in the pan. Watch carefully for any signs of burning.
- Puree the apricots by rubbing them through a fine sieve or food mill set over a bowl, or pulverize them in the jar of an electric blender. With a rubber spatula scrape them into a bowl.
- Add the vinegar, sugar, honey, paprika and salt and beat vigorously with a spoon or whisk until the mixture is smooth. Cover tightly and refrigerate until ready to use. (The sauce can be kept in the refrigerator for 2 or 3 months.).
- Spicy apricot sauce is traditionally served with white meat drumsticks but also may be used as a condiment with other fried or roasted meats and fowl.

## Nutrition Information

- Calories: 111
- Saturated Fat: 0
- Sodium: 101.9
- Fiber: 1.7
- Total Carbohydrate: 28.1
- Cholesterol: 0

- Protein: 0.8
- Total Fat: 0.2
- Sugar: 25.8

## 70. Spicy Curry Coconut Fried Red Snapper

*Serving: 6 serving(s) | Prep: 1hours | Ready in:*

## Ingredients

- 2 lbs red snapper fillets
- 14 ounces coconut milk
- 1 cup flour
- 1 tablespoon curry powder
- 2 teaspoons garlic salt
- 1/2 cup oil (for frying)
- lemon wedge (to garnish)

## Direction

- Cut fish into 12 pieces and marinate in the coconut milk for 1 hour.
- Heat the oil in a frying pan.
- Combine the dry ingredients in a bowl. Drain the marinated fish and coat with curried flour mixture.
- Carefully fry the fillets on both sides until golden brown and cooked through. Serve with lemon wedges.

## Nutrition Information

- Calories: 565.8
- Cholesterol: 71
- Fiber: 2.4
- Sodium: 121.6
- Sugar: 4.3
- Total Carbohydrate: 22.3
- Protein: 43.9
- Total Fat: 33.4
- Saturated Fat: 14.2

## 71. Spicy Marinated Bacon

*Serving: 2 lbs, 10 serving(s) | Prep: 20mins | Ready in:*

## Ingredients

- 2 lbs bacon, cheap is fine
- 1 cup Kikkoman soy sauce
- 1/4 cup tong of sriraha sriracha sauce
- 3 tablespoons oriental chili paste or 3 teaspoons vietnamese garlic and red chile paste
- 1 tablespoon granulated garlic omit if using the garlic chili

## Direction

- Pour everything except the bacon in a one gallon bag and mix well shake and knead way longer than you think.
- Place the bacon in the bag one slice at a time moving the bag to cover each slice with the marinade or they will stick together and not marinate.
- When there isn't enough marinade to cover any more bacon stop filling even if it's a little more or less than 2 lbs.
- Place in the refrigerator, turning every time you open the fridge. Marinate at least overnight up to a week. Over a week won't hurt the taste but the texture gets a little weird after a week or so.
- Grill very slowly. I prefer it slightly soft but you can crisp it up if you prefer.

## Nutrition Information

- Calories: 434.6
- Sodium: 2372.8
- Sugar: 0.5
- Total Carbohydrate: 2.4
- Cholesterol: 62
- Protein: 13.6
- Saturated Fat: 13.6
- Fiber: 0.3

- Total Fat: 41

## 72. Storm Smoothie

*Serving: 1 large smoothie, 1 serving(s) | Prep: 2mins | Ready in:*

### Ingredients

- one cup blueberries
- 1 fresh coconut (water and silky white flesh)
- 2 tablespoons non fat plain Greek yogurt
- 2 tablespoons raw flax seeds
- 1/2 cup pomegranate juice
- 1 ounce dark chocolate

### Direction

- Throw everything in your blender and enjoy!

### Nutrition Information

- Calories: 1724.7
- Sugar: 41.1
- Sodium: 103.6
- Fiber: 46.2
- Total Carbohydrate: 91.2
- Cholesterol: 0
- Protein: 20.8
- Total Fat: 156.8
- Saturated Fat: 127.9

## 73. Strip Steak Polynesian

*Serving: 4 serving(s) | Prep: 1hours | Ready in:*

### Ingredients

- 4 tablespoons soy sauce
- 2 teaspoons honey
- 2 garlic cloves, minced
- 4 (6 ounce) steaks (strip steaks)

### Direction

- Combine first 3 ingredients.
- Marinate the strip steak in the mixture for approximately one hour in the refrigerator.
- Place the marinated strip steak on the grill. Close the lid.
- Grill for 3 minutes, open grill, add the rest of the marinade sauce to the top of the steaks. Close the lid.
- Grill until cooked to desired doneness. Serve on a bed of rice.

### Nutrition Information

- Calories: 570.4
- Saturated Fat: 16.6
- Sodium: 1121.4
- Fiber: 0.2
- Total Carbohydrate: 4.3
- Cholesterol: 115.5
- Total Fat: 42.4
- Protein: 40.7
- Sugar: 3.2

## 74. Tahiti Po'e

*Serving: 4 , 4 serving(s) | Prep: 20mins | Ready in:*

### Ingredients

- 2 kiwi fruits, fresh
- 1 pineapple, fresh
- 1 orange, fresh
- 2 tablespoons brown sugar
- 2 tablespoons white rum
- 1/2 orange, peel of
- 1/2 lemon, peel of
- 1/2 cup orange, juice
- 1/2 cup grapefruit, juice
- 2 1/2 tablespoons cornstarch

### Direction

- Peel and thinly slice pineapple. Peel and quarter kiwis, remove white parts and cut green parts into small cubes.
- Peel and filet orange, keeping the juice.
- Mix fruits with sugar, rum, orange and lemon peel, set aside.
- Mix 5 tablespoons of fruit juice with starch, heat rest of the juice and stir in the dissolved starch.
- Bring to a light boil, add fruits and let simmer for about 10 minutes.
- Pour into 4 serving bowls, let cool and chill for 3 hours.
- Serve with desired garnish.

## Nutrition Information

- Calories: 240.5
- Total Fat: 0.6
- Fiber: 6.2
- Protein: 2.6
- Cholesterol: 0
- Saturated Fat: 0.1
- Sodium: 5.9
- Sugar: 39
- Total Carbohydrate: 57.5

## 75. Tahitian Chicken

*Serving: 8 serving(s) | Prep: 2hours | Ready in:*

## Ingredients

- 2 lbs chicken, cut up
- 1/4 cup soy sauce
- 1 piece peeled and grated fresh ginger
- 1/4 teaspoon pepper
- 1/8 teaspoon salt
- 1 small onion, minced
- 1 small garlic clove, minced
- 3 tablespoons brown sugar, packed
- 1 (8 3/4 ounce) can pineapple chunks, drained and juice reserved
- 1/2 cup orange juice
- 2 teaspoons cornstarch
- 1/4 cup water
- 1 (11 ounce) can mandarin oranges, drained
- 4 cups cooked rice or 4 cups cooked ramen noodles

## Direction

- Arrange chicken in a single layer in ungreased 13"x9" bake pan or Dutch oven, sprinkle with salt and pepper; set aside.
- Combine soy sauce, ginger, onion, garlic, brown sugar, reserved pineapple juice, and orange juice; pour over chicken. Cover and refrigerate 1 hour or overnight.
- Preheat oven to 350. Turn chicken and bake covered for 30 minutes. Uncover, and bake 20 to 25 minutes more, until golden or juices run clear or thigh pieces cook to 160 with meat thermometer.
- Remove chicken to a platter and keep warm.
- Skim fat from pan drippings. In a medium saucepan, combine cornstarch and water with pan juices; heat until thick and bubbly. Add pineapple and oranges and warm through; pour sauce and fruit over chicken. Serve with cooked rice or ramen noodles.

## Nutrition Information

- Calories: 442.8
- Sodium: 621.9
- Fiber: 1.5
- Total Carbohydrate: 45.4
- Cholesterol: 85
- Total Fat: 17.5
- Saturated Fat: 5
- Sugar: 15.5
- Protein: 24.9

## 76. Tahitian Sweet Potatoes With Fei (bananas)

*Serving: 6 serving(s) | Prep: 10mins | Ready in:*

## Ingredients

- 3 large sweet potatoes, peeled and diced
- 2 tablespoons cooking oil
- 1 (13 1/2 ounce) can light coconut milk
- 1 -2 tablespoon red curry paste
- 1 lime
- 1 tablespoon fish sauce
- 1 tablespoon brown sugar
- 3 firm bananas (they can be slightly green)
- 3 -4 Thai red chili peppers, sliced
- 2 tablespoons chopped cilantro

## Direction

- In a large saucepan, heat oil.
- Add potatoes and cook until lightly browned on the outside.
- Add coconut milk, curry paste, juice of the lime, fish sauce, and brown sugar to pan, stirring to mix well.
- Cover and simmer for 15 minutes or until potatoes are tender, stirring occasionally.
- Peel and slice bananas into chunks and stir in with the potatoes.
- Cook over low heat 5-7 minutes or until heated through and bananas have softened but are still intact.
- Garnish with chopped cilantro and sliced chilli peppers before serving.
- Serve hot.

## Nutrition Information

- Calories: 170.6
- Total Carbohydrate: 32.1
- Cholesterol: 0
- Protein: 2.3
- Total Fat: 4.9
- Saturated Fat: 0.7
- Sodium: 271.2
- Fiber: 4.1
- Sugar: 13.6

## 77. Tahitian Tuna (Poisson Cru)

*Serving: 8-10 serving(s) | Prep: 20mins | Ready in:*

## Ingredients

- 2 1/4 lbs tuna, cut into bites sized cubes
- 8 limes, cut in half
- 2 tomatoes, coarsely diced
- 1 small red onion, thinly sliced
- 1 small cucumber, thinly sliced
- 1 coconut, opened meat taken out and shredded
- 1 dash salt

## Direction

- Place tuna cubes into a large bowl and sprinkle with salt. Take the limes squeeze them over the tuna (make sure no seeds end up in the bowl).
- After add all of the juice from the 8 limes, stir the tuna until it is coated with the juice.
- Allow the tuna/ lime mixture to cook/ cure for about 5 minutes. (The lime juice actually begins to 'cook' the tuna).
- After the mixture has 'cooked' add the diced tomatoes, red onion and cucumber to the bowl and mix well.
- Take the freshly shredded coconut and place in cheesecloth, squeeze the coconut over the tuna (this is the coconut cream).
- Mix the tuna, vegetable, cream mixture refrigerate until ready to serve.

## Nutrition Information

- Calories: 218.6
- Protein: 30.8
- Total Fat: 6.5
- Saturated Fat: 1.6
- Cholesterol: 48.5
- Total Carbohydrate: 10.5
- Sodium: 73
- Fiber: 2.6
- Sugar: 2.9

## 78. Taste Of The Islands Banana Foster Trifle

*Serving: 4 desserts, 4 serving(s) | Prep: 30mins | Ready in:*

## Ingredients

- 1 (10 3/4 ounce) package frozen pound cake, thawed
- 1 (8 ounce) can pineapple chunks in juice
- 1 (3 1/2 ounce) packageinstant coconut cream pudding and pie filling or 1 (3 1/2 ounce) packagebanana cream pudding and pie filling
- 1 cup heavy whipping cream
- 1/3 cup sour cream
- 1/4 cup powdered sugar
- 4 tablespoons coconut rum, divided
- 1 cup caramel topping
- 3 bananas, thinly sliced
- 2/3 cup shredded coconut, toasted
- 1/3 cup macadamia nuts, finely chopped

## Direction

- Cut pound cake into 1-inch cubes. Set aside.
- Drain pineapple; reserving juice.
- Place pudding mix, whipping cream, sour cream, sugar, reserved pineapple juice and 2 tablespoons of the coconut rum in a large bowl.
- Beat at medium-high speed with an electric mixer until stiff peaks form.
- Combine remaining 2 tablespoon of coconut rum and ice cream topping in microwave-safe bowl. Microwave on High until warmed.
- Layer pound cake cubes in 4 Martini or dessert glasses.
- Drizzle caramel topping mixture over pound cake.
- Top with coconut cream mixture and bananas.
- Garnish with pineapple tidbits, toasted coconut and macadamia nuts.

## Nutrition Information

- Calories: 1095.5
- Saturated Fat: 29.1
- Sodium: 638.8
- Sugar: 28.6
- Total Carbohydrate: 138.1
- Protein: 9.9
- Total Fat: 57.6
- Fiber: 7.5
- Cholesterol: 136.8

## 79. Thai Curry Seafood Bruschetta

*Serving: 4 serving(s) | Prep: 15mins | Ready in:*

## Ingredients

- 2 tablespoons olive oil
- 1 1/2 cups diced plum tomatoes
- 1 tablespoon fresh ginger, minced
- 3 garlic cloves, minced
- 2 (15 ounce) cans coconut milk
- 1 1/2 tablespoons red curry paste
- 3 lbs assorted seafood
- 1/4 cup fresh cilantro, chopped
- salt

## Direction

- In large pot, heat olive oil over medium high heat. Add tomatoes, ginger, and garlic, and sauté for 1 minute. Add coconut milk and curry paste, stir well, and bring to a boil. Add seafood and lower heat to a simmer. (It may be necessary to add seafood a little bit at a time, judging by how fast it cooks - please see the info at the end) Simmer until seafood is done. Add cilantro or parsley, stir well, and served with crusty bread of your choice.
- The following are guidelines on roughly how long my seafood took to cook:
- 5-7 minutes.
- Large clams.
- Large scallops.
- Large shrimp.
- 3-5 minutes.

- Fish (flounder, tilapia, etc.), cut into 1-2" pieces.
- Smaller shrimp.
- Bay scallops.
- Mussels.

## Nutrition Information

- Calories: 502.8
- Protein: 6.8
- Total Fat: 46.2
- Saturated Fat: 35.9
- Total Carbohydrate: 22.2
- Cholesterol: 0
- Sodium: 115.5
- Fiber: 5.8
- Sugar: 15.5

## 80. Tickled Pink Tropical Island "iced Tea"

*Serving: 1 cocktail | Prep: 5mins | Ready in:*

## Ingredients

- 1/2 ounce Captain Morgan's spiced rum
- 1/2 ounce gin
- 1/2 ounce vodka
- 1/2 ounce tequila
- 1/2 ounce Cointreau liqueur or 1/2 ounce triple sec
- 1 1/2 ounces fresh lime juice
- 3 ounces guava nectar (such as Kearns)
- 3 ounces club soda (or to taste)
- ice, to serve
- lime wedge, to garnish

## Direction

- Pour all the ingredients into a large, tall 10-14 oz ice-filled Collins style glass.
- Top with the club soda and gently stir.
- Garnish with as many fresh lime wedges as you like, and a pink straw for sipping.

- VARIATIONS:
- Long Island Iced Tea: Replace the spiced rum with white rum and the guava juice with orange juice and the club soda with cola.
- Miami Iced Tea: Replace the spiced rum with white rum and the guava juice with orange juice and the club soda with cola and the Cointreau with blue curaçao.
- New England Iced Tea: Replace the spiced rum with white rum and the guava juice with orange juice and the club soda with cranberry juice.

## Nutrition Information

- Calories: 83.8
- Saturated Fat: 0
- Sodium: 20
- Sugar: 0.8
- Total Carbohydrate: 3.9
- Protein: 0.2
- Fiber: 0.2
- Cholesterol: 0
- Total Fat: 0

## 81. To Die For Coconut Pie! (New Zealand)

*Serving: 1 pie/cake, 4-6 serving(s) | Prep: 10mins | Ready in:*

## Ingredients

- 4 eggs
- 1 cup caster sugar
- 100 g unsalted butter, softened
- 100 g slivered almonds
- 1 cup desiccated coconut
- 2 tablespoons lemon rind
- 2 tablespoons orange rind
- 1/2 cup lemon juice
- 1/2 cup orange juice
- 1 cup coconut milk
- 1/2 cup plain flour, sifted

## Direction

- Preheat oven to 180 degrees.
- Place the eggs, sugar, butter, almonds, coconut, lemon and orange rind and juice, coconut milk and flour in a food processor or blender and mix until well combined. It should be reasonably runny.
- Pour into a buttered 28cm pie plate. Bake for 1 hour until lightly browned.
- Set aside to cool.
- Serve with cream, yoghurt or ice-cream, warm or chilled.

## Nutrition Information

- Calories: 1030.9
- Saturated Fat: 32.4
- Sodium: 162.9
- Fiber: 6.5
- Total Carbohydrate: 124.7
- Cholesterol: 239.8
- Total Fat: 55.7
- Sugar: 100.5
- Protein: 15.4

## 82. Tropical Carrot Layer Cake With Island Icing

*Serving: 1 frosted 3-layer cake, 12-16 serving(s) | Prep: 1hours45mins | Ready in:*

## Ingredients

- TROPICAL CARROT LAYER CAKE
- 1 1/2 cups softened unsalted butter (plus more for pans)
- 2 cups raw coconut sugar crystals (Coconut Secret)
- 2 1/2 cups all-purpose flour (plus more for pans)
- 2 1/2 teaspoons baking powder
- 1 1/4 teaspoons baking soda
- 1 teaspoon salt (omit if using salted butter)
- 1 teaspoon allspice (or 1/3 tsp each cinnamon, cloves, nutmeg)
- 1/2 teaspoon ginger powder
- 4 large beaten eggs
- 1 (6 ounce) container pina colada yogurt (Yoplait)
- 1/4 cup natural coconut rum
- 1 teaspoon pure vanilla extract
- 2 1/4 cups grated peeled carrots
- 1 cup baker's angel flake coconut
- 1 pureed medium very ripe banana (reserve 2 tablespoons)
- 1 (8 ounce) canwell-drained crushed pineapple (reserve juice)
- 1 cup roasted macadamia nuts (2/3 c chopped, 1/3 c ground)
- ISLAND ICING
- 24 ounces softened real cream cheese
- 1 cup unsalted butter
- 1 (16 ounce) packagesifted confectioners' sugar
- 2 tablespoons pureed ripe bananas
- 1 tablespoon lime juice
- 2 teaspoons pineapple juice
- 1 1/2 teaspoons natural coconut rum (not coconut extract)
- 1/2 teaspoon pure vanilla extract
- 1 small pinch salt
- SUGGESTED GARNISH
- 1/3 cup ground macadamia nuts (sides, from divided portion above)
- 1/3 cup baker's angel flake coconut (or more, top of cake)
- 1 tablespoon fresh carrot (curls or shreds, top center of cake)
- 1/4 teaspoon finely grated fresh lime peel (flecks, top of cake)

## Direction

- (BAKING NOTES: AVOID 9-INCH CAKE PANS WHICH HAVE LEFT AND RIGHT SIDE HANDLE TABS, MAKING IT IMPOSSIBLE TO FIT THREE 9-INCH PANS ON ONE BAKING RACK, WHICH IS RECOMMENDED FOR PROPER RISING AND EVEN BAKING. HERE IS A GUIDE FOR VARIATION BAKING TIMES AT 350°F:

Two 8 x 1-1/2-inch round baking pans -- 35 to 40 minutes Two 9 x 1-1/2-inch round baking pans -- 30 to 35 minutes Two 8 x 8 x 2-inch baking pans -- 25 to 35 minutes Two 9 x 9 x 2-inch baking pans -- 25 to 35 minutes -- One 13 x 9 x 2-inch baking pan -- 30 to 35 minutes One 15 x 10 x 1-inch baking pan -- 25 to 30 minutes Cupcakes (half full of batter) -- 18 to 23 minutes). (STEP ONE): PLACE oven rack in center position; PREHEAT oven to 350°F; OIL three (9-inch) cake pans lightly; PRESS a sheet of parchment paper into the bottom of both cake pans: SCORE parchment paper around bottom perimeter of cake pan; CUT a circle from scored sheet; LINE the bottoms of cake pans with parchment paper cut-out; BUTTER top of parchment paper insert well; DUST the greased inserts lightly with flour; TAP out excess flour; SET prepared pans aside.

- PULSE 1 cup pre-roasted macadamia nuts in a food processor and save 2/3 cup for the cake and set aside; COARSELY grind remaining 1/3 cup macadamia nuts in processor for the garnish, transfer to separate small bowl and set aside; PEEL enough fresh carrots to yield 2 1/4 cups grated; SHAVE a few 3-4 inch strips from carrots using a vegetable peeler and place into ice water for the garnish; FINELY grate the remaining carrots using a food processor grate to yield 2 1/4 cups (remove any large chunks that may get in), transfer grated carrots to a large bowl; ADD 1 cup Baker's Angel Flake coconut to carrots in bowl; PUREE one medium very ripe banana in food processor; ADD all but 2 tablespoons of banana puree to carrot mixture (reserving 2 tablespoons banana puree for the icing); RESERVE juice from one (8 ounce) can crushed pineapple; ADD well-drained crushed pineapple to carrot mixture in bowl; BLEND the carrot/coconut/banana/pineapple mixture well and set aside until needed; FOLLOW the link if candied carrot curls are desired, courtesy of The Cupcake Project (with thanks): http://www.cupcakeproject.com/2010/04/candied-carrot-curls-unique-carrot.html.

- MIX the following dry ingredients together in a separate medium bowl: 2 1/2 cups all-purpose flour, 2 1/2 teaspoons baking powder, 1 1/4 teaspoons baking soda, 1 teaspoon salt (omit if using salted butter), 1 teaspoon ground allspice (or 1/3 tsp each cinnamon, cloves, nutmeg), and 1/2 teaspoon ginger powder; SET aside.
- CREAM 1 1/2 cups (3 sticks) unsalted butter in a large mixing bowl using an electric stand mixer until light and fluffy; ADD 2 cups Coconut Secret brand Raw Coconut Crystals gradually to the creamed butter and beat well; CRACK 4 eggs into a separate container and remove any shell fragments; LIGHTLY beat eggs without adding to mixture.
- ALTERNATELY beat in the dry flour mixture and pour beaten egg mixture in one fourth increments on medium-low speed, until all of the flour mixture is used and all egg has been beaten into mixture; STOP mixer; ADD one 6 ounce container Yoplait pina colada yogurt, 1/4 cup natural coconut rum and 1 teaspoon pure vanilla extract; MIX on lowest speed; SLOWLY add the carrot/coconut/banana/pineapple mixture while beating on medium speed (without over-mixing); RAISE standing mixer top and scrape attachment and bowl sides; REMOVE bowl from stand; FOLD in 2/3 cup coarsely chopped roasted macadamia nuts.
- DIVIDE batter equally into the 3 prepared pans; DROP each cake pan levelly onto countertop 3 times to disperse air pockets; PLACE cakes into oven; SET timer for 30 minutes; BAKE until timer sounds; TEST center(s) of cake(s) with a wooden toothpick or cake tester until it comes out clean (bake for an additional 5 minutes and test again); REMOVE baked cakes from oven; LEAVE the cakes in pans to rest and cool for 10 minutes; CAREFULLY invert and transfer cakes from pans onto cooling racks, peeling away parchment paper; ALLOW cakes to cool completely; ZEST one fresh lime to yield 1/4 teaspoon and set aside; SQUEEZE juice from lime to yield 2 teaspoons for the icing.

- INTO a small cup using a fork to blend, mix 2 tablespoons banana puree, 1 tablespoon lime juice, 2 teaspoons reserved pineapple juice, 1 1/2 teaspoons natural coconut rum, and 1/2 teaspoon pure vanilla extract; SET mixture aside; INTO a large mixing bowl add 12 ounces softened real cream cheese and 1 stick softened butter over; BEAT until creamy; SCRAPE the mixture of banana, juices, rum and extract into the mixing bowl; BEGIN beating; SIFT in the powdered sugar while beating constantly until smooth; SLOWLY pour in the reserved blend the ISLAND ICING until smooth and creamy.
- PLACE one cake layer top-side up on cake plate or cake stand; SPREAD about 2/3 cup of the ISLAND ICING on the first layer of cake; PLACE the second cake layer top-side down evenly over first; REPEAT procedures to the third layer top-side up again; FROST the sides of the cake first with the ISLAND ICING; COVER the top layer of cake loosely with plastic wrap; TOSS 1/3 cup ground macadamia nuts along the sides of the cake; REMOVE wrap from unfrosted top cake layer.
- FROST the top of the cake with the remaining ISLAND ICING, decorating in swirls (Note: Any leftover icing freezes well if stored in an airtight container then defrosted in refrigerator); SPRINKLE the top of the cake with 1/3 cup flaked coconut; GARNISH top with 1 tablespoon finely grated fresh carrot and a few flecks of fresh lime zest; REFRIGERATE for an hour to set icing before serving.
- CUT servings and place onto plates; TEMPER cake servings to room temperature, covered loosely with plastic wrap (OR) WARM cake uncovered in a microwave defrost setting just long enough to soften cake and temper frosting; SERVE and enjoy!

## Nutrition Information

- Calories: 996
- Total Carbohydrate: 75.6
- Protein: 10.5
- Total Fat: 73.7
- Sodium: 658.3
- Sugar: 48.6
- Saturated Fat: 40.1
- Fiber: 4.1
- Cholesterol: 226.2

## 83. Tropical Crock Pot Chicken

*Serving: 6 serving(s) | Prep: 10mins | Ready in:*

### Ingredients

- 2 1/2-3 lbs boneless skinless chicken breasts, can use thighs, can use a combo of pieces
- 20 ounces canned pineapple tidbits, drained
- 1/2 cup chopped scallion, white and light green parts
- 1/4 cup chopped red bell pepper (optional)
- 2 tablespoons Dijon mustard
- 1 -2 tablespoon soy sauce
- 2 garlic cloves, minced
- 1/2 teaspoon tarragon
- 1/4 teaspoon pepper
- 1/4 teaspoon paprika
- salt, if needed to taste

### Direction

- Place the chicken pieces on the bottom of your slow cooker.
- In a bowl, mix together all remaining ingredients.
- Evenly pour over the chicken.
- Cover and cook on low for 5-8 hours (depending on the chicken parts used) or cook on high for 3-4 hours.

## Nutrition Information

- Calories: 273.2
- Saturated Fat: 1.1
- Total Fat: 5.3

- Sodium: 446.4
- Fiber: 1.8
- Sugar: 9.6
- Total Carbohydrate: 14
- Cholesterol: 121.1
- Protein: 41.5

## 84. Tropical Rice Salad With Mango Sesame Dressing

*Serving: 4-6 serving(s) | Prep: 10mins | Ready in:*

### Ingredients

- 1/2 cup rice
- 1/2 cup pineapple, cut in pieces
- 1/2 cup papaya, chopped into pieces
- 1 cup corn kernel, blanched
- 1 red bell pepper
- 1 green bell pepper
- 1/2 cup bean sprouts
- 1/2 cup water chestnut
- 4 scallions, thinly sliced
- 1/4 cup raisins
- DRESSING
- 1/4-1/2 cup mango puree
- 3 tablespoons peanut oil
- 1 teaspoon sesame oil
- 1 tablespoon soy sauce
- 1 teaspoon gingerroot, finely chopped
- 1 garlic clove, finely chopped

### Direction

- Cook rice in a pan of boiling, salted water about 12 minutes on medium heat. Make sure rice is just tender, not completely soft. Drain well and rinse with cold water. Drain Again.
- Mix together next 7 ingredients (pineapple through water chestnuts). Add rice to pineapple mixture and combine well. Season to taste with salt and pepper.
- Blend mango puree, garlic, ginger, and soy sauce on medium speed in blender (or by

hand, mix well). Slowly pour oil into top of blender, while running, until emulsified. If doing by hand, add oil in a slow stream while mixing constantly.
- Once combined, pour dressing over rice mixture and serve.

## Nutrition Information

- Calories: 314.8
- Saturated Fat: 2
- Sugar: 13.4
- Cholesterol: 0
- Protein: 5.4
- Total Fat: 12
- Sodium: 261.8
- Fiber: 4.7
- Total Carbohydrate: 50.3

## 85. Tropical Sorbet Terrine

*Serving: 12 serving(s) | Prep: 20mins | Ready in:*

### Ingredients

- 1 cup sweetened flaked coconut
- 1 pint coconut sorbet, softened
- 1 pint raspberry sorbet, softened
- 1 pint mango sorbet, softened

### Direction

- Preheat oven to 350 degrees.
- Line a 6 cup (8 1/2" x 4") loaf pan with a long strip of plastic wrap, leaving a 2" overhang on the long sides. Set aside.
- Spread coconut on a rimmed baking sheet.
- Toast in oven, tossing occasionally, until golden, 8-10 minutes.
- Let cool completely.
- Sprinkle 1/2 c toasted coconut in prepared loaf pan. Dollop coconut sorbet on top and spread evenly.

- Sprinkle that layer with 1/4 c toasted coconut. Repeat with raspberry sorbet and remaining 1/4 c toasted coconut, then mango sorbet.
- Fold plastic overhang over sorbet and freeze until firm, at least 8 hours, and up to 2 weeks.
- To serve, unfold plastic and invert onto a serving platter. Remove plastic and slice with a serrated knife.

## Nutrition Information

- Calories: 38.8
- Sodium: 20.3
- Fiber: 0.3
- Sugar: 3.4
- Total Carbohydrate: 3.7
- Saturated Fat: 2.4
- Protein: 0.2
- Total Fat: 2.8
- Cholesterol: 0

## 86. Volcano Cocktail

*Serving: 2 serving(s) | Prep: 5mins | Ready in:*

## Ingredients

- 6 ounces grapefruit juice
- 2 ounces fresh lime juice
- 3/4 ounce maple syrup
- 1/2 ounce simple syrup
- 3 ounces demarara rum or 3 ounces golden rum
- 2 ounces jamaican rum or 2 ounces dark rum
- 1 ounce hawaiian rum or 1 ounce white rum
- 1/2 ounce Bacardi 151 rum (optional)

## Direction

- Shake ingredients (except 151 rum) with ice, then strain into volcano bowl or cocktail glasses.
- Pour 151 rum into volcano crater if using volcano bowl, and ignite just prior to serving.

## Nutrition Information

- Calories: 268.5
- Saturated Fat: 0
- Sodium: 3.8
- Sugar: 16.1
- Total Carbohydrate: 19
- Cholesterol: 0
- Total Fat: 0.1
- Fiber: 0.2
- Protein: 0.6

## 87. Watermelon Mai Tai

*Serving: 4-8 serving(s) | Prep: 5mins | Ready in:*

## Ingredients

- 500 g peeled watermelon, chopped
- 125 ml pineapple juice
- 125 ml white rum
- 60 ml triple sec
- 1 teaspoon grenadine
- crushed ice, to serve

## Direction

- Place the watermelon, pineapple juice, rum, liqueur and grenadine in the jug of a blender and blend until smooth.
- Divide the ice among serving glasses.
- Pour over watermelon mixture to serve.

## Nutrition Information

- Calories: 135.1
- Total Fat: 0.2
- Fiber: 0.6
- Sugar: 13.3
- Total Carbohydrate: 17
- Cholesterol: 0
- Protein: 0.9
- Saturated Fat: 0

- Sodium: 3.5

## 88. Tongan Papaya

*Serving: 2 halves, 2 serving(s) | Prep: 1mins | Ready in:*

## Ingredients

- papaya
- coconut milk

## Direction

- Halve and seed a papaya.
- Fill cavity with coconut juice.
- Wrap in banana leaves or tinfoil if you're short on the above.
- Bake slowly.
- Takes on a totally different flavor.
- You'll love it.

## Nutrition Information

- Calories: 0
- Sodium: 0
- Fiber: 0
- Sugar: 0
- Total Carbohydrate: 0
- Saturated Fat: 0
- Protein: 0
- Total Fat: 0
- Cholesterol: 0

# Index

# Conclusion

Thank you again for downloading this book!

I hope you enjoyed reading about my book!

If you enjoyed this book, please take the time to share your thoughts and post a review on Amazon. It'd be greatly appreciated!

Write me an honest review about the book – I truly value your opinion and thoughts and I will incorporate them into my next book, which is already underway.

Thank you!

If you have any questions, **feel free to contact at:** *author@hugecookbook.com*

Kara Quinn

hugecookbook.com

Made in the USA
Monee, IL
19 May 2024